THE ROCK PAINTINGS OF THE CHUMASH

1 ft.

A pictograph from the San Emigdio Mountains, Kern County (KE-2).

THE

ROCK PAINTINGS
OF THE CHUMASH
A Study of a California Indian Culture

Written and Illustrated by Campbell Grant

With a Foreword by Robert F. Heizer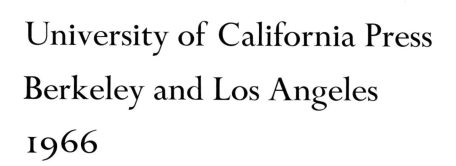

University of California Press

Berkeley and Los Angeles

1966

University of California Press
Berkeley and Los Angeles, California

Cambridge University Press
London, England

Second Printing, 1966

A grant from the Santa Barbara Museum of Natural History
to assist in the publication of the illustrations is gratefully acknowledged

Designed by Harry Marks

Manufactured in the United States of America

TO THE MEMORY OF

Dr. V. L. VanderHoof, 1904-1964

WITHOUT HIS ENTHUSIASM AND

SUPPORT THIS BOOK WOULD NEVER

HAVE BEEN WRITTEN

Foreword

A felicitous and successful combination in the person of the artist and author, Campbell Grant, and the remarkable painted cave art of the Chumash tribe of the Santa Barbara region have produced this book, which is the first of its kind in the field of aboriginal North American prehistoric art.

The Chumash tribe (actually a number of politically and geographically distinct groups who are collectively called a tribe because each spoke a dialect of a single language) occupied the pleasant and bountiful coast, its hinterland, and the northern off-shore islands of the Santa Barbara region. They were a large population living in permanent villages and subsisting on ocean products (fish, mollusks, and sea mammals) and land resources (deer, acorns, and roots). The popular image of the California Indians as degraded, cultureless, and bestial people, which the Americans of the Gold Rush period created, has long been known to anthropologists as misleading and untrue. Whoever has read *Yurok Narratives* told by Robert Spott, or Mrs. Alfred Kroeber's *Ishi* or *The Inland Whale* will understand that the intellectual attainments and world view of California Indians (no less than those of other primitive peoples who have been objectively studied) mark them as extraordinarily interesting examples of humanity.

The Chumash appeared to the Spaniards in 1769, when Portolá's expedition visited and described them, as superior to the Indians they had seen to the south in northern Mexico, along the Colorado River, and in the Mohave Desert. Father Crespí wrote that they were "of good figure and disposition, active, industrious and inventive," and Father Font characterized them as "extremely intelligent and skillful, alert and rather bold." The "superiority" of the Chumash in their attitudes and behavior which attracted the notice of the eighteenth-century Spaniards is recognizable also in their tools, implements, and ornaments made of stone, bone, and shell, which the archaeologist of the present day recovers from the deposits of debris which mark their former village sites. In perfection of shape and finish, durable items of prehistoric Chumash material culture are notably the results of craftsmanship and care superior to those which most of the other California Indians were capable of or interested in producing. Of basketry and wood objects made by the Chumash there are a few examples preserved, these also being superlative examples of pre-industrial technology. Of the undoubtedly rich body of folklore, mythology, ritual, and the like, there has come down to us scarcely anything, and this is especially unfortunate because this class of knowledge in the intellectual sphere would provide us some kind of conceptual background into which we could project the truly remarkable painted cave art of the ancient Chumash. We are, therefore, left only the resource of speculation about who made the paintings and what they may have meant. I am satisfied that Campbell Grant is correct in attributing the paintings to shamans or medicine men, the tribal practitioners of magic. The paintings are quite obviously more than mere decoration; they can only have been symbolic and religious in meaning. Although some of the caves were lived in, apparently most of them were not so used. The painted recesses, therefore, were probably shrines, or shaman's retreats, or places for the performance of ritual acts which involved the application of painted designs to the walls.

Why the paintings were made and what the various designs and figures originally meant we will never know. The author's suggestion that individual differences in artistic ability can be demonstrated is, I believe, a sound one which the evidence supports.

There is no evidence that "impersonating cults" in which a costumed and masked human became, with the wearing of the disguise, the god or spirit itself, obtained among the Chumash, but the lack of information does not prove that such cults may not have been once present. The swordfish headdresses recovered archaeologically along the Santa Barbara coast may indicate the practice of masking. The "antennae" which are attached to the top of the heads of life forms (as at sites V-1, V-7, and SL-5)[1] may be representations of prayer plumes of the sort that were commonly stuck in the hair by the Maidu, Miwok, Patwin, and Pomo tribes of north central California on ritual occasions. If this were the case, one might infer additionally that some of the quadruped life forms which seem to be animals could in fact represent costumed humans. The reader who has seen the engraved and painted representations of the part-animal, part-human "sorcerers" of the cave of Trois Frères in France will perhaps agree. Whatever the meaning of the painted figures and designs may have been, it seems likely that most of them had exact significance only in the minds of these prehistoric peoples of the sort that ordinary artifacts, like arrowpoints, stone pots, and bone awls, do not illustrate, and they are therefore important in enlarging our knowledge of the prehistoric Chumash people's occult and esoteric

[1]See p. 101 for an explanation of site listings.

beliefs and practices. In an approximate way, the discovery of the large numbers of Chumash rock paintings makes us aware of a dimension of thought hitherto unsuspected, in much the same way that the discovery of the European cave art of the Paleolithic period showed us that the art of painting was known much more anciently in human history than could have been imagined, and that the Paleolithic cave artists were aesthetically sophisticated to an extraordinary degree.

I believe, with the author, that the Chumash (archaeologically referred to as Canaliño) were the people who painted all or most of the cave art that now is to be found within the territorial limits of the Chumash tribe. This question could not be answered beyond any doubt unless we had some early historical record, but the author's arguments for the relative recency of the paintings are most convincing. It is possible that radiocarbon dating of charcoal from campfires in the refuse deposits of caves or shelters that also bear paintings (for example, site SB-17) will tell us whether the Chumash or an earlier people camped in these spots. Since many of the cave earths are dry, one might even find paintbrushes or bits of pigment in the soil which would serve to associate the radiocarbon dated levels of occupation with the time of actual painting of the walls. I have some confidence that careful archaeology in the limited number of painted caves which were lived in, aimed at determining the age of the Canaliño painted pictographs, could be successful. Further, I will hazard the guess that if and when the paintings are dated they will be shown to have been made in the last thousand years.

The four mounted horsemen (almost certainly Spaniards) from site LA-1 are done in profile rather than the usual "spread-eagled" convention, and almost certainly postdate the accompanying painted elements on the walls of this cave. Chumash cave painting, like the petroglyphs of California and Nevada, apparently represent an activity which had largely, perhaps even wholly, gone out of vogue by the time the Spanish destroyers made their appearance in the late eighteenth century.

Mr. Grant's volume on the culture of the Chumash, their remarkable painted parietal art, and his broader discussion of pictographic art in the New World is a very substantial contribution to the study of primitive art, a solid addition to California archaeology, and a well-deserved tribute to one of the most interesting aboriginal tribes of North America, the Chumash. His investigation is most timely since it assures permanent recording of the cave paintings, an important matter in a state which has already lost many of its archaeological resources through thoughtless destruction and lack of public appreciation.

Robert F. Heizer

Acknowledgments

So many people have helped me on this project that, in any attempt to list them all, some may inadvertently have been left out. For special information on sites and permission to visit ranches and closed areas, I am especially indebted to Gene Bingeman, Mrs. William Cooper, Edwin Dethlefsen, Walter Fiegus, Mrs. Duncan Jackson, J. G. James, Robert Jones, Louis Lundsberg, Howard W. Mansfield, Carson Miles, W. S. Palmer, Dibblee Poett, Juan Romero, Clarence Ruth, Warren Stockton, Edna Tenney, Carl Twisselman, Mr. and Mrs. William Washburn, and Robert Woods.

For technical help in providing pictures and source material, I wish to thank Carl Dentzel of the Southwest Museum; William E. Hinchliff of the Santa Barbara Public Library; David Gebhard, fellow student of rock painting, University of California at Santa Barbara; and especially Clifton F. Smith, librarian of the Santa Barbara Museum of Natural History, who cheerfully endured my endless questions and requests for a full year.

I am particularly indebted to the late Dr. V. L. VanderHoof, director of the Santa Barbara Museum of Natural History, and to trustees Harold S. Chase, Hilmar O. Koefod, Irving Wills, and Preston Webster for their constant support and interest.

I greatly appreciate the critical reading of the manuscript by these specialists in the study of California Indians: Robert F. Heizer, University of California, Berkeley; James Deetz, University of California, Santa Barbara, and Phil C. Orr, Santa Barbara Museum of Natural History.

I am grateful for the help of Barbara Lawrence, Dorothy McLatchy, and Margaret Ortel, who typed their way through the various drafts—from the first

ACKNOWLEDGMENTS

disreputable mass of erasures and second second thoughts to the ultimate elegance produced by the electric typewriter, double-spaced. I was fortunate in having the sharp eye and unerring good judgment of editor Grace Buzaljko to see the manuscript through the final stage.

My warmest thanks to these *compañeros* who scrambled through the brush and along the trails with me: Dennis Breedlove, Henry Brown, Theodore Carpenter, Marcus Cravens, John Cushing, Joseph Doctor, Nicholas Goodhue, John Hamilton, Albert Heimlich, John Hickok, Wales Holbrook, Eben McMillan, the Curtis Newmans, Glenn Reitz, Richard Smith, Edward R. Spaulding, William J. Thompson, and particularly to my good friends, the Homer Wadkins and the Jack Cawleys, who have led me to many new sites, and to my patient family, who have not only put up with my periodic obsessions but have furnished my chief assistance: Gordon, my oldest son, an expert with the machete who has hewn out miles of trail in the chapparal country, and my youngest, Douglas, a tireless rock climber who has saved me many a perilous and usually fruitless climb.

Contents

CONTENTS

Illustrations

ILLUSTRATIONS

ILLUSTRATIONS

PLATES

Introduction

If you were to center a pair of dividers on the bleak, windswept island of San Miguel off the Santa Barbara coast, and describe a quarter-circle 100 miles long from north to east, you would encompass the land of the Chumash. These Indians, once so numerous, have now vanished, leaving the remains of their hundreds of villages for the pick and shovel of the archaeologist and a wealth of splendid artifacts for the museums and the pothunters. The most spectacular achievement of the Chumash is scarcely known. In the wind-scoured sandstone outcrops of the back country are thousands of caves, and many of these are decorated with rock paintings. The paintings range in size from a few feet to over 40 feet in length, and in technique from simple line drawings in red to very complex polychrome designs in six colors.

The early explorers and the missionaries have left us no accounts of these decorated caves. Their work was along the fertile coastal plain and in the valleys, while the paintings, or, more properly, pictographs, are almost without exception in remote mountain locations, well hidden from the curious by the trailless, precipitous, and chaparral-covered terrain.

The earliest investigator of the Chumash pictographs was the Reverend Stephen Bowers, who sketched two sites near San Marcos Pass in 1877. The first published notice of the Santa Barbara area pictographs was in Garrick Mallery's pioneer work, *The Pictographs of the North American Indians* (1886). He described six sites in the Chumash country. Except for a few scattered magazine articles and Myron Angel's flight of fancy, *La Piedra Pintada*, in 1910, there was no further mention until Julian Steward's excellent *Petroglyphs of California and Adjoining States* in 1929. This work was based on the records of the Univer- 1

INTRODUCTION

sity of California and had descriptions of both petroglyphs (rock peckings or carvings) and pictographs (rock paintings). Steward listed eighteen sites in the Chumash area.

In 1935 the Santa Barbara Museum of Natural History under the direction of D. B. Rogers made a survey of the caves in the remote Hurricane Deck country of the San Rafael Mountains and brought out reports of numbers of painted sites. These were the nucleus of the project, begun in 1960, that has led to the publication of this book.

I worked two seasons recording known sites and exploring for new ones, and saw over seventy painted areas. The field work entailed travel by car, truck, jeep, horse, and on foot—mostly the latter with a good deal of machete work in trail-making through almost impenetrable chaparral.

In order to have some understanding of the paintings, it is essential to know as much as possible about the people who painted them. It seems fairly certain the pictographs are the work of the Chumash—the people who were here when the Spanish arrived in 1542. For this purpose, I undertook to write a sketch on the history and culture of the Chumash. The more I read on the subject, the more fascinated I became, until the sketch is now the major part of the book. I make no excuses for this "tail wagging the dog," as I discovered that there is no single book available that tells the full story of these extraordinary Indians.

CHAPTER ONE

The Land

The country of the Chumash was very large. It included all of Santa Barbara County, most of Ventura County, and parts of San Luis Obispo, Kern, and Los Angeles counties—in all about 6,500 square miles. Kroeber outlines the territory in his *Handbook of the Indians of California* (1925, p. 551):

> They held the three northern large islands of the Santa Barbara archipelago—Anacapa does not appear to have been inhabited permanently. They clustered thickly along the calm shore from Malibu Canyon westward to Point Concepción and from there extended northward along the more boisterous and chillier coast as far as Estero Bay. Inland in general, they reached to the range that divides the direct ocean drainage from that of the great valley; except that in the west their frontier was the watershed between the Salinas and the Santa Maria and short coastal streams; and in the east, some small fragments spilled into part of the most southerly drainage of the San Joaquin-Kern system. The Carrizo Plain is doubtful as between the Chumash and Salinan and may not have contained any permanent villages.

The country is largely mountainous, including these coastal ranges: the Santa Ynez, San Rafael, and Sierra Madre mountains and part of the Santa Monica, Caliente, and Temblor ranges. These average about 3,000 feet in elevation, though individual peaks in Ventura County are nearly 9,000 feet. The mountain masses are broken by a few large valleys: the drainages of the Santa Clara, Ventura, Santa Ynez, and Santa Maria Rivers, the barren Carrizo Plains, and the narrow intermittent coastal shelf between Point Concepción and Point Mugú.

Rainfall is slight. The average at Santa Barbara is 18 inches a year. In the mountains the rainfall and snow are much heavier, while the lack of rain in the

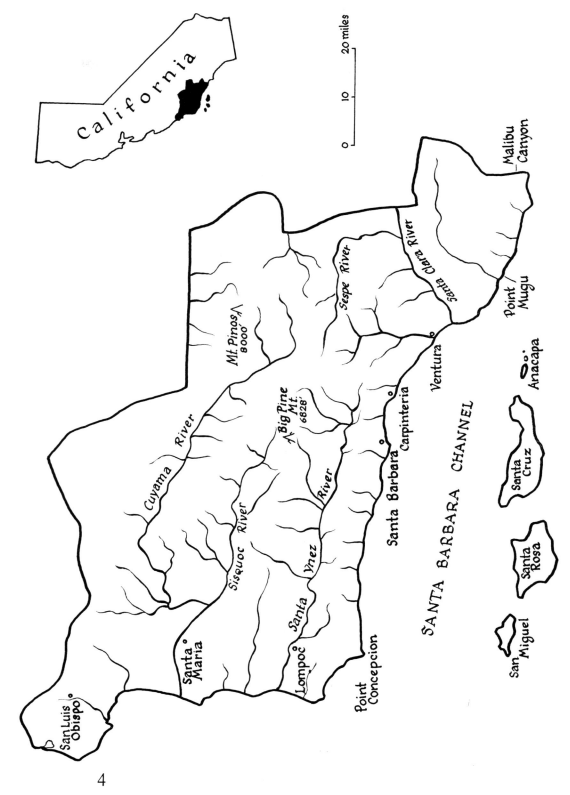

FIGURE 1. The area occupied by the Chumash in southern California. All names on the map are present-day names. (After Kroeber, 1925)

4

FIGURE 2. The San Rafael Range looking north from Mt. Figueroa. Many of the pictographs occur in this remote region. (From a painting by Ray Strong for the Santa Barbara Museum of Natural History)

interior valleys has created semi-desert conditions. The rainy season lasts from November to May, and by midsummer most of the streams are becoming dry. However, nearly all the creeks maintain a year-round flow at their headwaters because of the springs in the mountains. The coastal plain is famous for its mild climate; tempered by sea breezes and fogs, it seldom rises over 80° F. in the summer or below freezing in the winter. In the interior valleys, the weather is more severe, with the thermometer often dipping close to zero and going above 110 degrees.

Most of the Chumash country is made up of Pleistocene, Tertiary, and Cretaceous sandstones, shales, and conglomerates with interbedded volcanic rocks, principally basalt. Occasionally there are outcrops of older rocks such as serpentine, dense sandstone, and slaty shales. The only granite rocks occur in the higher country—the San Emigdio Mountains and adjacent mountains to the south.

The Santa Barbara Channel Islands, San Miguel, Santa Rosa, Santa Cruz, and Anacapa, lie offshore at distances from 11 to 30 miles. From the mainland, on a clear day, they look like a rugged mountain range rising from the sea. The islands are chiefly of volcanic rock and were once a continuation of the Santa Monica Mountains, where much basaltic rock occurs.

With the exception of bleak, waterless Anacapa, the islands once supported a large Indian population. The largest island is Santa Cruz, where steep cliffs line the north shore and peaks rise over 2,400 feet. It is the most heavily wooded of the islands, with oak, Bishop pine, and the endemic Santa Cruz Island pine predominating.

The rare and spectacular Island ironwood, *Lyonothamnus floribundus asplenifolius*, occurs on both Santa Cruz and Santa Rosa. The mammal life is confined to foxes, skunks, mice, bats, and lizards, and along the shore there are many sea

5

FIGURE 3. West end, Santa Cruz Island. (From a painting by Ray Strong for the Santa Barbara Museum of Natural History)

FIGURE 4. Typical terrain between San Luis Obispo and Morro Bay. (From a painting by Ray Strong for the Santa Barbara Museum of Natural History)

lions. The sea otter was abundant in Chumash times. Santa Rosa is not so precipitous and is mainly grassland with stands of oak, Torrey pine, and Bishop pine. San Miguel, the windswept, most westerly island, is visited by immense herds of sea lions and sea elephants.

The plant life of the mainland is rich and varied. In the foothills and in the mountains grow the impenetrable chaparral thickets of manzanita, chamise, ceanothus, yucca, sumac, and many other tough, drought-resistant plants. In the high country are the coniferous forests of yellow pine, Jeffrey pine, Coulter pine, big-cone spruce, white fir, and incense cedar. At lower levels are the piñon and Digger pines and juniper. On the *potreros*, or high grasslands, in the valleys and canyons, and along the coastal plain are oaks of many varieties to furnish acorns, the staple food of the Chumash. Along the streams are willow, alder, maple, laurel, and sycamore trees.

6

The larger animal life of the mainland includes the black bear, mule deer, mountain lion, fox, coyote, and badger. In Chumash times the savage grizzlies were abundant but had been hunted out of the region by the 1890's. The last stand of the majestic California condor, largest North American bird, is being made in the heart of the Chumash territory—some sixty individuals are known to occupy certain mountain areas. Both the golden and the bald eagle are found along the channel and in the mountains. Mountain and valley quail are abundant through the region, and pigeons and doves come to the coast and inland valleys in the fall.

The richest animal life available to the Indians was the sea mammals, whales, porpoises, seals, and sea otters. These, together with the infinite variety of fish and shellfish in the channel, provided an inexhaustible food supply.

It is small wonder that the Chumash chose to live in such a land. It was a fine place to live. It still is.

CHAPTER TWO

The People—History

It is difficult to get a clear picture of the Chumash. As Kroeber put it (1925, p. 551), "There is no group in the State that once held the importance of the Chumash concerning which we know so little". Our knowledge of these vanished Indians comes from three main sources: the journals and diaries of the Spanish explorers, the record books of the missions, and the mass of artifacts taken from the burial grounds in recent times.

The Explorers

The recorded history of the Chumash begins on October 10, 1542. On that day, Juan Rodríguez Cabrillo, sailing up the coast in search of a northern strait to Europe, anchored his two small ships, the *San Salvador* and the *Victoria*, off the present site of Ventura. He landed near a Chumash village and took possession of the country. A diarist of the expedition, Juan Paez (see Bolton, 1925, p. 25), wrote:

> Here there came to the ships very many canoes, each of which held twelve or thirteen Indians; they told them of Christians that were going about in the interior. They indicated by signs that in seven days they could go where the Spaniards were.

This may have referred to the gold hunter Coronado, who had spent the two previous years following the trail of the Seven Golden Cities of Cibola to a dead end on the Kansas plains. Hernando de Alarcón had led a maritime party up the Colorado as far as the present site of Yuma, and it was probably this group that the Chumash described. On the 14th, Cabrillo's men made a landfall off Carpintería (Bolton, *ibid.*, p. 26):

> On the following Saturday they continued on their course . . . anchoring in front of a magnificent valley densely populated, with level land, and many groves. Here came canoes with fish to barter; the Indians were very friendly . . . all the way there were many canoes . . . and many Indians kept boarding the ships. They pointed out the pueblos and told us their names.

Cabrillo visited many points on the mainland and on the Channel Islands. He died on the island of San Miguel that winter, as the result of a fall, and was probably buried there.

The next European contact was in 1602 when Sebastian Viscaíno cruised up the coast, exploring and mapmaking. The devout Viscaíno had the habit of naming conspicuous geographic features after the saint on whose day he happened to see them. Accordingly, on December 4, St. Barbara's feast day, when he entered the great channel formed by the offshore islands and the mainland, he promptly named it the Santa Barbara Channel. Continued bad weather and strong winds made landing difficult, and contact with the natives was slight. The journal of Father Ascensión (*ibid.*, p. 118) gives this example of the generosity and friendliness of the natives:

> After we left the port of San Diego (also named by the saint-conscious Viscaíno) we discovered many islands placed in a line one behind the other. Most of them were inhabited by many friendly Indians who have trade and commerce with those of the mainland. It may be that they are vassals of a petty king who came with his son from the mainland in a canoe with eight oarsmen to see us and to invite us to go to his land saying he would entertain us and provide us with anything which we needed and he possessed. There are many people in this land, so many that the petty king, seeing that there were no women on the ships, offered by signs to give everyone ten women apiece if they would all go to his land, which shows how thickly populated it is.

After the brief visit of Viscaíno, the peaceful life of the Chumash went on undisturbed for 167 years. The Indians north of Mexico had proved a terrible disappointment to the Spanish. The people to the east were warlike and had no gold; the Californians were friendly but had no gold either. All the expeditions had been a great drain on the royal purse and lesser private purses. As a result, the country north of the Gulf of California was written off as a poor investment, unworthy of the close attention that Spain had given to Mexico and Peru.

By 1768 a new element had entered the picture. The Russians, established in Alaska and busily engaged in killing Aleuts and sea otters, began to look south and now posed a threat to the Spanish claims on the Pacific. The Viceroy felt that it was time to establish an outpost at Monterey Bay, a fine harbor described by Viscaíno. In 1769 a land expedition under the leadership of Captain Gaspar de Portolá left San Diego, where Junípero Serra had just founded the first mis- 9

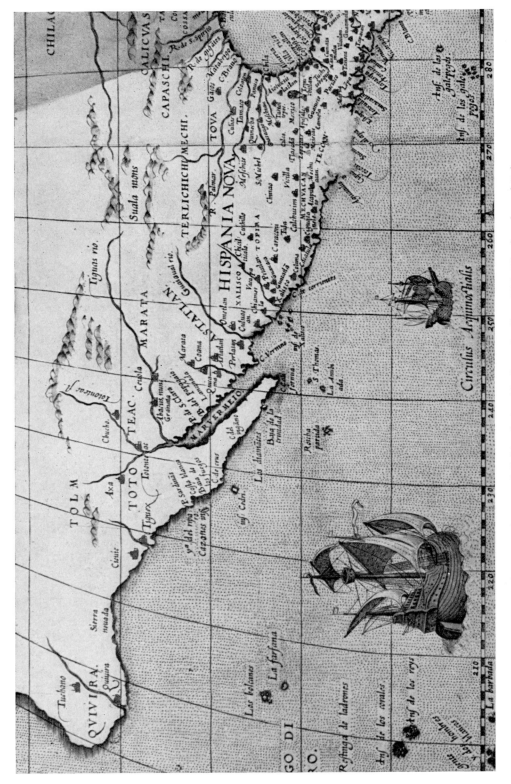

FIGURE 5. A very early map of California by Abraham Ortelius, 1570. The location of Baja California is fairly accurate, but north of the peninsula all is fanciful. Tiguex, the Indian settlement seen by Coronado in the Rio Grande Valley, is shown on the coast, while the mythical kingdom of Quivira appears to the northwest and will be included in all maps until late in the eighteenth century. Note the Sierra Nevada, located roughly where it will later be found. (Earnest Watson collection)

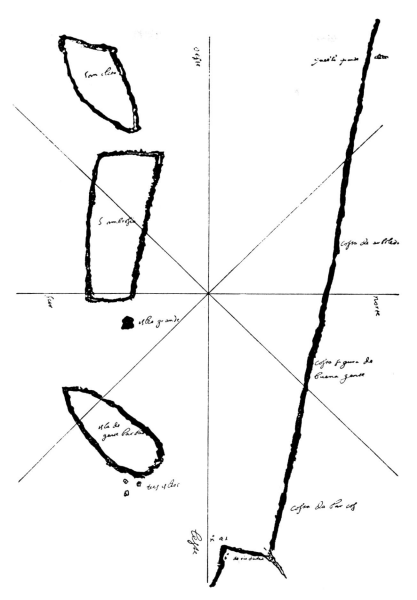

FIGURE 6. The first map of the Santa Barbara Channel, drawn in December, 1602, by Father
Antonio de la Ascención, diarist of the voyage of Sebastian Viscaíno. Southeasterly gales
prevented the Spanish from landing, and the map is consequently rather sketchy. Explanation:
The islands, reading down, are *San Anicleto* (San Miguel), *San Ambrosio* (Santa Rosa), *isles
grande* (refers to the big islands and not to the ink blot), *islas de gente barbas* (island of the
bearded people, Santa Cruz), *tres isles* (segments of Anacapa). The coastal names reading
down, are *pueblo grande* (big town, probably Dos Pueblos or Mescaltitlán), *costa de arboledo*
(wooded coast, Montecito and Carpintería valleys), *costa segura de bueno gente* (safe coast
of the good people), *costa de barcos* (coast of the boats, Ventura–Rincón), (*punta*) *de rio dulce*
(point of the fresh-water river, Point Mugú and the Santa Clara River). (After Wagner, 1929)

11

sion. The party consisted of Portolá, Lieutenant Pedro Fages, the engineer Miguel Constansó, the friars Juan Crespí and Francisco Gómez, and a small number of leather-jacketed soldiers. From the journals kept by Fages, Crespí, and Constansó, we get the best descriptions of the Chumash in their natural state. On August 16, they camped on Rincón Creek at the edge of the Carpintería Valley. Father Crespí noted that day (Bolton, 1927, pp. 162–163) that:

> As soon as we arrived all the people came to visit us and brought a great supply of roasted fish until the canoes arrived with fresh ones . . . afterwards they brought us an abundance of bonitos and perch. A few miles to the west was a town of 38 houses. Not far from the town we saw some springs of pitch. The Indians had many canoes and at the time were building one, for which reason the soldiers named the town La Carpintería . . .

Passing the present site of Santa Barbara, the party was constantly followed by crowds of Indians pressing them with gifts of fish until ". . . it was necessary to tell them not to bring any more for it would eventually have to spoil" (*ibid.*, pp. 167–168). At the same locality Lieutenant Fages wrote, "The gentleness and good disposition of the Indians gives good reason for entertaining a moral certainty of their reduction, provided they be preached the word of God" (Fages, 1937, p. 26).

The Missionaries

As the expedition passed through this happy land, the sands were running out for the carefree Chumash. Portolá returned from the North (he had failed to recognize Monterey Bay from Viscaíno's description and, going farther, discovered San Francisco Bay). He found that the log cabin mission Serra was struggling to maintain was in desperate straits. The Indians had proved uncoöperative and were supplying very little food. A supply ship came in the spring when the Spanish were on the point of giving up the venture, and in June Serra sailed for Monterey (Portolá had found it on a later attempt in May) to establish the second mission, San Carlos de Monterey. With this we have the start of the mission system that eventually included twenty-one missions and was to prove so fatal to the coastal Indians of California.

Father Junípero Serra was an extraordinary man. He was born in Mallorca, as was Crespí, who studied under him at the monastery of San Francisco. He came to Mexico in 1749 and became active in the missions of Baja California when the Jesuits were removed in 1767. He had exceptional administrative ability, and was tireless in his drive for unredeemed souls. The glowing descriptions, given by explorers, of countless friendly Indians along the California coast drew Serra irresistibly northward. After the long bloody record of Spanish and Indian warfare in the New World, this was almost too good to be true.

His road was not easy. There was constant conflict with the military authori-

12

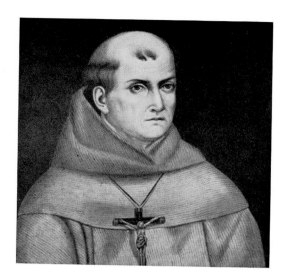

FIGURE 7.
Father Junípero Serra.
(Bancroft Library)

ties over mistreatment of Indian women by the soldiers. This in turn led to uprisings and some killings. It was a year before the San Diego mission had a single convert, and by 1773 the five missions had baptized only about five hundred Indians, mostly women, children, and old people. One of these missions was that of San Luis Obispo, the first to be founded in Chumash territory. Food was always short and dependent on the tenuous sea connection with Mexico. To put the colonies on a better footing. Captain Juan Bautista de Anza conducted two overland expeditions, the first to find a land route to Upper California, and the second, in 1775, to bring in families from Sinaloa to settle the new country. They brought the sheep and cattle that were the beginnings of the great herds of the rancho days. The diarist of the second expedition was Father Pedro Font, a shrewd observer, whose book-length account is a classic of western travel.

esta ocasion las demarqué segun la fachada que hacian
desde este paraje de la Assumpta, y es la que aqui pongo:
y observé que mirando al sur desde dicho paraje, la Ysla
mas grande, que es la de la Santa Cruz, caia al sud-
este, y las demas se venian siguiendo de ella hasta el sur,

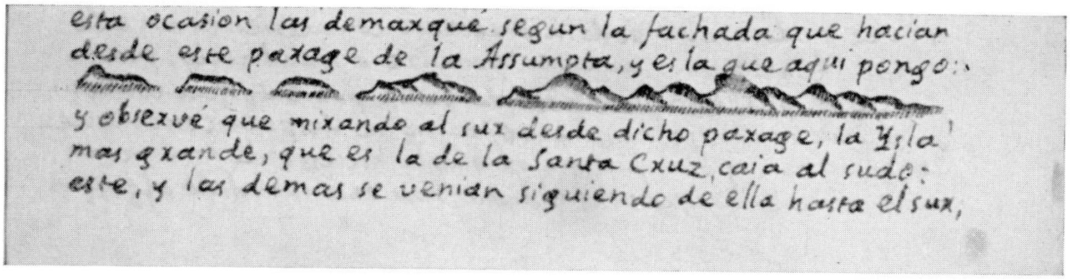

FIGURE 8. Profile of Channel Islands (largest is Santa Cruz) as seen from the Assumpta (Ventura) River. From the original manuscript journal of Father Pedro Font (1775). (John Carter Brown Library, Brown University)

Anza's successful trip with the settlers and cattle was the turning point in the growth of the missions. They began to be self-supporting. Permanent buildings were started, and in 1782 Serra at last obtained permission from Spain to start his long-cherished plan to build a complex of missions in the Chumash country. As Father Palou, Serra's close associate, wrote, "[we] . . . journeyed along the Santa Barbara Channel and rejoiced to find there so many pagans upon whom

the light of our holy faith was about to dawn" (Rogers, 1929, p. 9). That year the mission San Buenaventura was founded and a presidio started at Santa Barbara. Governor Neve, who detested the mission system, was able to block the founding of the other channel missions until shortly before Serra's death in August, 1784. It was two more years before his successor, Fermín Francisco de Lasuén, erected a cross at the site and founded the mission of Santa Barbara. Before the month was out, three adults had been baptized, "known respectively in paganism as Catayu, Siocr, and Mumiyaut" (*ibid.*, p. 10). The last two mis-

FIGURE 9.   The reception of Count Jean François Galaup La Pérouse at Monterey in 1786. One of the three padres is Father Fermín Francisco de Lasuén, Serra's successor. This is the first picture of California mission Indians. (Museo Naval Collection, Madrid)

sions established in the Chumash area were La Purísima Concepción, 1787, and Santa Inés, 1804. The records at the Santa Barbara mission are very complete and will form the basis of the account of the mission period. The pattern at the other four missions is remarkably similar.

Building began at once, and aqueducts to bring water from the mountains miles away were started. By midsummer, seventy Indians had been baptized and dressed in mission clothing: for the men, a pair of breeches and a shirt; for the women, a chemise and skirt, these to be issued every six months. By 1789, 307 neophytes were camped around the mission. To establish the mission economy, the Indians were taught all the basic trades, such as woodworking, tilemaking, stone masonry, leather and iron working, weaving, animal husbandry, and agriculture. That same year, as the labor pool grew, the temporary buildings were replaced by adobe and tile construction, and as a sure sign of the dawn of civilization—the first jail was built. In the next few years, building began on adobe houses for the neophytes. These were surrounded by an eight-foot wall and the enclosure locked at nine o'clock each night. Of these houses, a mission historian (Englehardt, 1923, p. 67) rather smugly writes: "The Indians we can imagine, must have felt like lords in their neat and spacious homes which were so much more attractive and safe than the filthy huts they had inhabited as pagans."

In these safe and attractive new houses, the neophytes sickened and died. In daily contact with the Spaniards, they caught the white man's diseases. They died from syphilis. They died from measles. They died from chicken pox. With no immunity, their first common colds almost invariably went into pneumonia or tuberculosis. It has been estimated that the average life of the neophyte was six years. In 1798, after only thirteen years of mission activity, there were 864 living converts—662 had died, or over 40 per cent.

In August, 1792, the naturalist, Longinos Martínez, making a survey of natural resources for the Spanish government, spent a month in the channel area. A year later, Captain George Vancouver (who insisted on calling California "New Albion"), anchored off Santa Barbara, and his naturalist, Archibald Menzies,

FIGURE 10.   The earliest known picture of Santa Barbara, drawn by John Sykes from Vancouver's flagship *Discovery*, anchored offshore, 1793. a. Indian village; b. presidio; c. mission. (Bancroft Library)

a   b   c

15

wrote the first English account of the Chumash. The two naturalists give us a last good look at the Chumash before the complete destruction of their culture. Martínez notes a reason for the great success of the channel missionaries: "Although the Indians are warlike, skillful with the bow, intrepid and of a proud nature, their fixed domicile makes them accept the yoke of obedience and religion with greater readiness and constancy than do other nations" (Simpson, 1961, pp. 52–53).

Before the turn of the century, the system of peonage was established. Indians trained at the mission were loaned out to soldiers and settlers, any return for their labor going to the mission. The shiftless garrison at the presidio a mile away was a constant source of trouble to the padres and the Indians. The four presidios were each planned for a cavalry force of 250 soldiers, but when Menzies was in Santa Barbara in 1793 he reported the garrison as one lieutenant, two sergeants, and sixty to seventy soldiers. Forbes in 1839 wrote that California was the Botany Bay of Mexico and that the troops stationed there were made up largely of deserters, mutineers, and men guilty of military crimes. The presidios were originally established to protect the missions against the supposedly hostile Indians and to keep law and order. At Santa Barbara they were mostly employed in bringing back runaway neophytes who often tried to return to their

FIGURE 11. The presidio at Santa Barbara in the 1830's. (From A. Robinson, 1846)

old carefree life. The punishment was by shackles, the lash, and stocks, extremely hard things for the Indians to accept. Before the coming of the Spanish, they had few forms of punishment. The soldiers, supported entirely by Indian labor, were not altogether idle. The effect of almost fifty years of Spanish garrisons in an Indian community can be seen today in the large number of Spanish-speaking mestizos in the channel towns.

FIGURE 12. Santa Barbara mission in the 1830's. (From A. Robinson, 1846)

In 1801 a severe epidemic of pleuropneumonia swept the country and many of the Indians died. At the beginning of 1803, there were 1,792 Indians attending mass, the largest number ever assembled. The lowest death rate was recorded that year—38 per cent of the converts since 1786. In 1812 the mission church was partly destroyed by earthquake, but by 1820 the final building of adobe, stone, and tile was completed. A superb example of Spanish colonial architecture, it stands today, still under the control of the Franciscan order and looking much the same as when the Indians put the last tile in place. By 1812 there were very few of the early neophytes left alive. All the mission Indians had become syphilitic and the birth rate had fallen alarmingly. As the enslaved population dwindled, the constant demands on them for work became harder to bear. The happy people seen by the diarists had become spiritless and degenerate. The civilian population did their share in exploiting the captive Indians, and in 1813 Father Olbés sourly observed (Englehardt, *op. cit.*, p. 98):

> The people of the province known as the *gente de razón* (whites) are so lazy and indolent that they know nothing more than to ride horseback. Labor of any kind

17

they regard as dishonorable. They are of the opinion that only Indians ought to work; wherefore they solicit the services of the Indians for even the most necessary things for their maintenance such as cooking, washing, doing garden work, taking care of the babies, etc.

Driven to desperation by the mistreatment of the soldiers and the relentless benevolence of the padres, the remaining Indians attempted to revolt in 1824, and at the same time there were uprisings at the Santa Inés and La Purísima missions. The fighting was touched off by the flogging of a neophyte at the Santa Inés mission. The Indians, armed with bows and arrows, besieged the small Mexican garrison, and two Indians were killed. During the battle the mission was fired and many buildings were destroyed. The following day a relief party of soldiers from Santa Barbara lifted the siege and restored order. News of the fighting quickly spread to La Purísima mission, and the Indians seized the mission after the six soldiers surrendered. During the battle one neophyte was killed, and four travelers stopping by on their way to Los Angeles were murdered by the excited Indians. A month later a Mexican force of over one hundred soldiers armed with a cannon forced the surrender of the rebels, and in reprisal seven Indians were executed by Captain De la Guerra and twelve were given long prison terms.

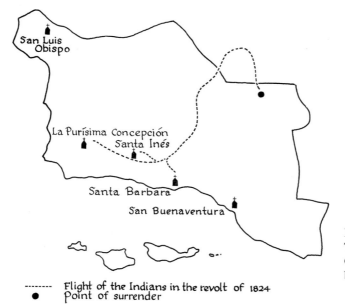

FIGURE 13.
The five missions established in the Chumash country by the Franciscans between 1772 and 1804.

-------- Flight of the Indians in the revolt of 1824
● Point of surrender

In Santa Barbara, the rebellion began as soon as the news came from Santa Inés and La Purísima. The neophytes armed themselves with bows and arrows and withstood a three-hour battle with De La Guerra's presidio troops. Three Indians were killed before the soldiers retired. All the neophytes then fled to the mountains behind the mission, and when the soldiers returned to the fray after their siesta only one Indian was seen, who had returned for some flour. This man they shot. The next day four old Indians from the Dos Pueblos ran-

18

FIGURE 14.
Captain José De la Guerra y Noriega, commandant of the Santa Barbara presidio during the Indian revolt of 1824. For many years he also served as *sindico* or treasurer for the Franciscan missions of California. (From the painting by Leonardo Barbieri, 1850, now at the Santa Barbara Historical Society)

cherías went to the mission to see what was going on and were promptly shot by the soldiers. There can be little doubt that the troops were relishing this break in the endless torpor of garrison life and, when permission was granted to sack the neophyte quarters, they did a thorough job. Appalled by these two outrages, the runaways decided not to return but to seek safety through the mountains to the San Joaquin Valley, where they hoped to establish a new home. Without the Indian slave labor, neither mission or presidio could survive, so a Lieutenant Fabregat and fifty soldiers were sent after the refugees. They were overtaken at Buena Vista Lake and a brief clash took place. The Indians fled to the San Emigdio hills, where they were joined by fugitives from Purísima and Santa Inés. Here the Mexicans (Mexico had broken her ties with Spain several years before) attacked them, killing four. Delighted at this victory, Fabregat hurried back to Santa Barbara, telling Commandante De la Guerra and Governor Argüello that high winds and dust clouds had made further pursuit impossible. The Governor ordered the pursuit to continue. The rebels were to be captured and returned to Santa Barbara at once. Father Sárria was forced to go on the expedition, as the authorities felt that a little soft talk from a padre might succeed if bullets and bayonets failed. The priests had refused to accompany Fabregat on his abortive chase, as they wanted no part in the bloody methods of the military. The whole affair had greatly upset the padres, who seemed sincerely to have the good of the Indians at heart. As Kroeber wrote (1925, p. 888):

> It must have caused many of the fathers a severe pang to realize, as they could not but do daily, that they were saving souls at the inevitable cost of lives. And yet such was the overwhelming fact. The brutal upshot of missionization, in spite of its kindly flavor and humanitarian root, was only one thing, death.

19

Two bodies of soldiers now converged on the unhappy Chumash, one group of 63 soldiers from Santa Barbara and another of 50 from Monterey. Each group had a cannon. They made contact with the fugitives in the San Emigdio hills, and a council was held. With fatal persuasiveness, Father Sárria convinced the Indians of the wisdom of returning to the bosom of the Church, and the first and last rebellion was over. Some of the Chumash did not return to the coast but settled in the San Joaquin, and some valley Indians were returned to Santa Barbara with the fugitives.

At the end of the year the rolls showed 923 Indians at the mission. That year marked the virtual completion of the main task of the mission—they were running out of pagan Indians. Even the Island Indians had come over and taken the road to extinction.

In the early 1800's the Russians were harvesting otters on the Channel Islands. Their Aleut hunters were armed with guns and doubtless killed many of the islanders for sport or to steal their furs.

In 1827 the Mexican government took the first step in the long-contemplated secularization of the missions. The mission Indians were declared free—free to go and become those thrifty, ambitious, self-supporting farmers the padres had trained them to be. The decree was meaningless. Most of the Indians, now thoroughly dependent on the mission type of existence and their old village culture completely destroyed, chose not to go. They were like the prisoner who after fifty years in jail is told he may now go back into the world. Spiritless and confused, they clung to the fathers until the next blow fell.

In 1833 the secularization of the missions began, the vast holdings of the Church now coming under the control of the government. These holdings were not inconsiderable, and it is astonishing that the civil authorities had held off so long. In 1831 the Chumash missions owned the richest lands from San Diego to San Francisco. The livestock inventory is impressive (W. H. Davis, 1929, pp. 389–390):

> San Luis Obispo—60,000 cattle, many horses and sheep
> Santa Inés—20,000 cattle, 1,500 horses, 10,000 sheep
> La Purísima Concepción—20,000 cattle, 1,000 horses, 15,000 sheep
> Santa Barbara—20,000 cattle, 1,000 horses, 20,000 sheep
> San Buenaventura—25,000 cattle, 1,500 horses, 10,000 sheep

The missions were to become parish churches, half the property to go to the Indians and administrators to have charge of the remaining properties. Unfortunately, few of these administrators were either capable or conscientious, and, when the final liquidation was completed, the immense land holdings, including the Indians' share, had found their way into the hands of a few favored Mexicans, while the Indians lived on around the crumbling missions or found work on the big ranchos. In 1836, Richard Henry Dana rode up to the mission at Santa Barbara and wrote, "The Mission is a large and deserted looking place, the outbuildings are going to ruin and everything gives the impression of decayed grandeur" (Dana, 1941, p. 117).

Lesley Byrd Simpson (1962, p. 169) sums up the basic reason for the collapse of the missions, aside from the lack of Indians:

FIGURE 15. The Santa Barbara mission in 1875. The neophyte quarters are in the left background, and the buildings in front of the mission are the *mayordomo's* house and the tanning vats. (Photo by Watkins from the collection of the Huntington Library)

Under the Bourbon despotism as administered by the able Charles III, it was inevitable that he should consider the frontier missions his political instruments. The missions were, and were designed to be, supply depots for the military outposts, furnishing provisions, clothing, arms, and even men for the defense of the Province—a crushing burden for what were, after all, primitive subsistence farms, and the Indians met it with the only effective protest at their disposal, namely, by deserting or dying. When the Bourbon system fell to pieces under the impact of the French Revolution, the Napoleonic Wars, and the revolt of the American colonies, the missions no longer had political value, and in any case the new governments were too busy trying to survive, to support them. So the missions died.

With both the new and the old ways of life gone, the wretched Chumash declined further. In 1839, there were 246 of them left in the Santa Barbara area. In the space of a single lifetime a great Indian nation, one of the largest and most culturally advanced in California, had ceased to exist.

The Rancheros and the Gringos

The life on the great California ranchos of the 1830's and 40's was a fine, easy life. It was a time of roundups, barbeques, bear and bull fights, and fandangos. The ranchos were small feudal kingdoms, completely self-supporting but de-

21

pendent on the Boston trading ships for manufactured luxuries. Captain José de la Guerra y Noriega, long-time commander of the presidio of Santa Barbara, had at one time six ranchos totaling over 300,000 acres and with more than 50,000 cattle. These ranchos held many of the scattered Chumash in a state of peonage with little pay and no future. The old records of this period confine their mention of the Indians to notices of their drunkenness and disorders. This contrasts strangely with the accounts of the same Indians by the explorers before the benefits of civilization had arrived.

FIGURE 16.   Californians of the *ranchero* period. From *Exploration de Territoire de l'Orégon, des Californies et de la Mer Vermeille, Exécutée Pendant les Années 1840, 1841 et 1842*, by Duflot de Mofras. (California State Library)

The final chapter for these unhappy people now opened. For many years, a few Americans, or *gringos*, as the Spanish called them after the Mexican War, had been drifting into southern California, marrying into Spanish families, becoming Mexican citizens, and adapting themselves to the sleepy tempo of the country. In January, 1848, gold was discovered on the American River in eastern California, and the next month California came under the American flag, part of the prodigious spoils of our steamroller attack on Mexico. The trickle of American immigration became a steady stream and then an irresistible flood. The Johnny-come-lately gringos would soon show the native Californians a few lessons in land grabbing.

The vast herds of cattle held by the ranchos had previously gone into hides and tallow at about two dollars a head, but with the gold seekers' demand for meat the *hacendados* enjoyed a brief period of prosperity. But before the turbulent period was over, most of the great ranchos had fallen into Yankee hands by legal and other methods. Soulé, Gihon, and Nisbet, authors of *Annals of San*

22

Francisco (1854), who had arrived with the gringo tide, put the position of many Americans quite bluntly:

> Men feed the ox and the sheep for their milk and fleece, the hog for his flesh, the ass for the strength of his back, and all for their increase; so did the Fathers feed their Indian converts, and find abundant profit in their labor and personal services, whom they left, as they perhaps found . . . just as tame, dull and silly, dirty, diseased and stupidly obstinate as the other brutes named.
> But another race was destined soon to blow aside the old mists of ignorance and stupidity and to develop the exceeding riches of the land. . . . The Spaniards had scarcely proceeded any way in the great work . . . when the Anglo-Saxon, the true and only type of modern *progress*, hastily stepped in, and unscrupulously swept away both their immediate forerunners as effete workers, and the aborigines of the land, as lumberers and nuisances in the great western highway of civilization.

The final masters of California treated the Indians with complete contempt, lumping them all under the name of "Diggers." To the men who had crossed the prairies and fought the savage tribes along the way, the missionized Indians were a particularly poor, debased, and spiritless lot. Ironically, the coastal Chumash seem to have had a somewhat better life under their arrogant new masters, who ignored them, than under the Spanish, who had worked so hard to uplift them. At least the death rate declined somewhat.

The fate of the inland Chumash was somewhat different. Before the collapse of the mission system, ex-mission Indians and inland Chumash, under the pressure of encroaching whites, had been migrating to the southern San Joaquin Valley and joining semi-nomadic bands of Yokuts. As the enormous ranchos came into being, these bands began systematic raids to steal cattle and horses.

In *The Adventures of Zenas Leonard* (1839), there is a good account of the situation at this time. Leonard was a fur trapper with the Joseph Reddeford Walker exploring expedition that had crossed the country from Missouri to Monterey in 1833 and, after wintering in Monterey, were returning in the spring of 1834. Not far from the San Juan mission, they met a party of Mexicans in pursuit of Indians with stolen horses, and some of the trappers joined in the chase. An encampment was found where some old Indians with women and children were drying horse meat. All the Indians were killed and their ears cut off as proof for the priests and alcaldes that every effort had been made to recover the lost horses.

Walker's party then entered the San Joaquin Valley, following the Sierra Nevada foothills and looking for a pass through the mountains. They saw great numbers of Indians, and near the southeastern end of the valley they found a village of Spanish-speaking Indians practicing agriculture. This band, of between seven and eight hundred, were Chumash fugitives from the Santa Barbara missions who had fled in the revolt of 1824, and they showed the trappers a number of images they had taken from a mission church. They had easily adapted to a life on horseback and frequently raided the coastal ranches for remounts and 23 meat. Two of the Chumash were hired as guides and led the party to the break in the mountains known today as Walker Pass.

The Mexican punitive expeditions, though successful enough in handling women and children, were incapable of coping with the situation, and the stock raiding continued. It was not until the discovery of gold, followed by the movement of land-hungry settlers into the San Joaquin Valley, that the Indians were finally pushed back into the mountains or liquidated.

Where the Spanish had employed and absorbed the Indians through racial mixture, the Americans aimed at extermination or segregation in ghetto-like reservations. Governor Burnett in his message to the California legislature in January, 1851, said ". . . that a war of extermination would continue to be waged until the Indian race should become extinct, and that it was beyond the powers or wisdom of men to avert the inevitable destiny."

The settlers, continuing the frontier policy that "the only good Indian is a dead Indian," reacted savagely to Indian cattle raids. The usual ratio of reprisals was a wiped-out village—men, women, and children—for the theft of a cow.

In 1854, the government made a feeble attempt to stop the trouble by establishing a reservation at Tejón Pass. This at one time had a large Chumash population. Due to mismanagement and the usual misuse of funds, it was not a success and was not long continued. By the late 1880's, the valley Indians, Yokuts and the migrated Chumash, were largely wiped out and their culture destroyed. The decline of the coastal Chumash continued, due chiefly to disease and a low birth rate, and at the turn of the century only a handful remained. The last full-blooded Chumash was Ignacio Aquino Tomás, who died in 1952 and was buried at the Santa Barbara mission. At the present time, there is a small reservation in the Santa Ynez Valley of 75 acres where about 35 mixed-blood Chumash live. They are completely assimilated into the white community.

From 1770 to 1910, according to Kroeber, the California Indian population declined nearly 90 per cent. In the case of the Chumash, the decline was total. The survival of the Indians in California seems to have been in direct ratio to their distance from the mission influence.

The Archaeologists and the Pothunters

Civilized man has always taken more interest in the artifacts of primitive man than in primitive man himself. Having successfully buried the Chumash and his culture, the white man now began the long job of digging him up.

In the early 1870's, reports of aboriginal village sites and cemeteries filled with an abundance of fine artifacts in the Santa Barbara Channel region came to the attention of the Smithsonian Institution. In 1875 an expedition headed by Paul Schumacher was sent to the area by the Smithsonian Institution and the Peabody Museum to make a preliminary investigation. At the same time, Dr. H. O. Yarrow, leading an archaeological survey party in connection with the U. S.

FIGURE 17. Santa Barbara in 1873, shortly before the first scientific investigations by Yarrow, Schumacher, and Cessac into the vanished Chumash culture. (Bancroft Library)

Army Engineer survey west of the 100th meridian, set out for the same region. It was agreed that Schumacher would look into the islands and Yarrow would investigate the mainland. Their work on Santa Cruz, in the Goleta area, and at the Dos Pueblos sites, Mikiw and Kuyamu, turned up many artifacts, including a few wooden objects. Even fragments of the famous canoes were found. Almost fifteen tons of artifact material was removed by the Yarrow party.

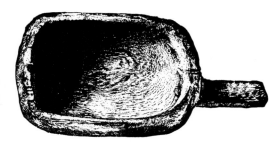

FIGURE 18.
Wooden ladle found by the Yarrow party. Length, 7 inches. (After Putnam, 1879)

A few years later, in the fall of 1877, a French scientific expedition headed by Alphonse Pinart and Léon de Cessac arrived in the channel. They had just come from a collecting stopover in Peru and were eager to explore the country described by the Spanish. Cessac spent the better part of a year in the Chumash area, coming into conflict with Schumacher, who had returned for another haul for the Peabody Museum. The American, with the assistance of the local authorities, obstructed Cessac's work and threatened to confiscate his collection, stating that there was a law prohibiting this sort of work by foreigners. This proved untrue, and the Frenchman returned to France with over 3,000 artifacts, now in the Musée de l'Homme in Paris. Cessac spent some time studying the Santa Barbara mission records and somehow managed to get a manuscript copy of Father Boscana's wonderful account of the Indian customs in the San Juan 25

Capistrano country, *Chinigchinich*. How Cessac was able to get this priceless account away from the padres is a mystery, but in a successful attempt to get around Schumacher's restrictions on the Burton Mound site (see below), he admits to having used "money, discretion and whiskey."

This was the last scientific work to be done in the Chumash country for nearly 50 years. Unhappily, the work of these early investigators had not gone unnoticed, and now the pothunters looking for relics to sell entered the scene. There was no mainland burial area of any importance they missed. The most indefatigable of these people was a curious man, the Reverend Stephen Bowers. Beginning his career in the east as a Methodist minister, he appeared in Santa Barbara in the middle 1870's and guided some of the early expeditions to the rich cemetery sites. A man of parts, he was a minister, a self-styled Ph.D., geologist, archaeologist, temperance lecturer, and country newspaper editor. This ecclesiastical scavenger posed as a scientist to mask his wholesale looting and boasted that he had been instrumental in the removal of over 30 tons of artifacts from the Santa Barbara area. No late Victorian felt culturally complete without a few Indian relics in his curio cabinet. To satisfy the demand, many lesser collectors labored beside Bowers in a prolonged plundering spree until the glutted market collapsed.

In 1923, J. P. Harrington, assisted by David Banks Rogers, excavated Burton Mound, site of a major village in Santa Barbara, for the Smithsonian Institution. Soon after, the newly formed Santa Barbara Museum of Natural History

FIGURE 19.   Recent archaeological excavation, Skull Gulch, Santa Rosa Island. Great care is taken to leave all bones and artifacts in position for photographing and measuring. The burials in the foreground have been radiocarbon-dated at 600 years. (Santa Barbara Museum of Natural History)

asked Rogers to make a detailed exploration of all known village sites in the area. The work continued for four years on the mainland and to some extent on the islands of Santa Cruz and Santa Rosa. Over one hundred sites were investigated and described in his book *Prehistoric Man of the Santa Barbara Coast.* His work indicated that the mainland had been occupied by three distinct peoples. The first, Rogers calls the Oak Grove People. Their settlements were invariably on high ground and usually in a wooded region. The villages were small and the houses dirt-banked, semi-subterranean huts, similar to some in use today in Siberia. The typical rectangular cooking stone was always present in the huts, and nearby were found large elliptical metates and oval, hand-size manos. These Indians made crude flint points, knives, and fist axes. Orr (1952, p. 213) noted these additional characteristics of the Oak Grove: prone burial and lack of weapons, ornaments, steatite, and asphalt. They were long-headed people, with an average cephalic index of 73.5. The brow was sloping and the teeth protruded. In Dr. Roger's opinion, these people were among the earliest on the continent and had lived along the channel at a period when it was far wetter than at present.

Several thousand years ago a new group, the Hunting People, appeared. Whether the Oak Grove People had already disappeared, were assimilated, or were driven out by the undoubtedly warlike Hunting People can only be conjectured. At any rate, the round-headed newcomers (average cephalic index 80.0), with Mongolian facial characteristics, now occupied the channel region. They made a great many fine flint projectile points. These people were excellent hunters, and in their refuse heaps are found the bones of deer, puma, black bear, and grizzly. No trace has been found of their dwellings, which might easily have been the skin and pole shelters of other semi-nomadic peoples. With the Hunting People, the interesting basket mortar and the mortar and pestle make their first appearance. These Indians did not use steatite (the nearest steatite quarries were on Catalina and could only be reached by the canoes of the later people), but the use of asphalt had begun with the basket mortar. The dead were no longer buried prone but flexed, head down.

By A.D. 1000 the whole region was in the possession of the Chumash, who had supplanted or amalgamated with the remnants of the Hunting People. In any event, the mesocephalic or medium-headed Chumash had taken over. The complex culture of these channel Chumash, Rogers calls Canaliño. Orr writes that the mortar and pestle became highly developed. Steatite and asphalt were extensively used, weapons were made with a higher degree of craftsmanship, and plank canoes make their appearance. The Chumash gradually spread out until they dominated the region shown on the map (fig. 1), which they held until the missionaries arrived. With their big planked canoes, they reached and settled the channel islands of Santa Cruz, Santa Rosa, and San Miguel. These people were only incidentally hunters; theirs was a food-gathering existence, and the gathering was good. With the endless variety of fish in the channel and with the oak groves to supply acorns for meal, it was an easy life. Further inland, hunting no doubt assumed much more importance in varying the basic acorn diet. 27

Rogers published his findings in 1929. The following year, R. L. Olson published his *Chumash Prehistory*. His conclusions are based on a shorter period of investigation but are much more specific than those of Rogers. Olson was less than enthusiastic about the channel Indians and wrote (1930, p. 20): "The material culture represented throughout, gives evidence of no remarkable developments beyond the bare needs of a rather drab existence . . ."

In 1943, Phil Orr of the Santa Barbara Museum of Natural History described the excavations on Mescaltitlán Island in the Goleta slough, slightly west of Santa Barbara. He found a superb burial of an important woman, with a great quantity of decorated material (see also p. 45). Since 1946, he has been doing intensive work in one area on Santa Rosa Island. His discoveries are very important and have radically changed some earlier ideas—one of which was that only the Chumash had inhabited the islands. The material at some sites occurs at depths of a few feet to nearly 40 feet, giving a unique opportunity to build a radiocarbon time scale. The earliest date for the Canaliño is 2,590 years ago. Underlying this, Orr records a Highland culture 5,370 years old which may relate to both the Canaliño and the Hunting People of the mainland. A still earlier culture 6,820 to 7,400 years old may correlate with the Hunting People (Orr, 1960, p. 7).

In 1961, human bones found in the same area at a depth of 37 feet below the surface, in beds containing bones of dwarf mammoth, were estimated to be 10,000 years old. There is only one older verified dating of human bones in the Western Hemisphere, and this is also a discovery of Orr's: In 1952, an 11,200-year-old partial skeleton was found in Fishbone Cave near Reno, Nevada (Orr, 1956a).

CHAPTER THREE

The People—Culture

Until very recently, all our knowledge of these Indians was based on studies of the coastal Chumash (Canaliño culture). Information on the interior was fragmentary and inconclusive. Kroeber in 1925 attempted a rough estimate of the boundaries of the Chumashan-speaking people. Of this estimate, he said, "... it must be frankly confessed that the lines there drawn ... represent little but conjecture based on topography" (1925, p. 552).

I have arbitrarily followed Kroeber's topographical boundaries of the Chumash country and, happily, new evidence is appearing that may prove his conjectures quite close to the mark. In 1961, J. F. Deetz and E. Dethlefsen excavated Alamo Pintado, a mountain village and burial ground north of the Santa Ynez River (unpublished MS) and found a characteristic Canaliño culture. As I was finishing this writing, a collection of artifacts was acquired by the Santa Barbara Museum from dry caves and a burial area south of the Cuyama River in northern Santa Barbara County. The collection contains examples of nearly all known Canaliño artifact types. It is becoming apparent that the culture pattern throughout the Chumash country was quite homogeneous, though reaching its greatest perfection and complexity along the channel.

Physical Appearance

It is unfortunate that none of the artists that visited California in the late 1700's and early 1800's made a single drawing of a Chumash Indian. There is no contemporary drawing in existence of these Indians in their native state. The Spanish diarists thought the Chumash superior to any other California tribes and happily have written many vivid descriptions of them. Paez, in 1542, wrote: "They were dressed in skins and wore their hair very long and tied up with long strings interwoven with the hair, there being attached to the strings many gewgaws of flint, bone and wood," (Bolton, 1925, p. 27). He thought little of the island Indians and noted that "They live very swinishly and go about naked", (*ibid.*, p. 34). The men of the mainland, according to later observers, went naked except during cold weather, but the women always wore some kind of skirt. Font, too, noted the lack of clothing (Bolton, 1930, p. 250):

> The dress of the men is total nakedness. For adornment they are in the habit of wearing around the waist a string or other gewgaw which covers nothing . . . Some of them have the cartilage of the nose pierced, and all have the ears perforated with two large holes in which they wear little canes like two horns as thick as the little finger . . . in which they are accustomed to carry powder made of their wild tobacco . . . These Indians are well formed and of good body although not very corpulent on account of their sweating, I judge. The women are fairly good looking.

Another diarist found them " . . . well built and of a good disposition, very agile and alert and ingenious to a degree" (Fages, 1937, p. 25). He must have seen them during a cold spell, as he added: "The men go clothed with a large cloak made of the skins of cony, hare, fox, and sea otter; the garment reaches the waist, the captains only being allowed to wear it reaching to the ankle . . ." (*op. cit.*, p. 32). The captains were the owners of the canoes and people of importance in the village. For additional warmth, the men wore a cloak or blanket made by twisting strips of bird or rabbit skin and weaving these strips together. The men sometimes carried a netting around the waist which served to carry odd objects.

FIGURE 20.
Chumash man and woman, based on early accounts. The man carries a shinny stick and ball. The woman has a gaming tray and an asphaltum lined water basket.

In 1793 the Scotsman Menzies (1924, p. 315) observed:

> These natives appeared to be of a middling stature with mild features, thin lips and in general were more delicately formed than those we saw about the Settlements to the northward; their hair is long and black and most of them wore it in a bunch gathered on the crown of their head.

Martínez, the naturalist, was quite taken by the women after seeing the shaggy squaws in Baja California and wrote enthusiastically (see Simpson, 1961, pp. 53–54):

> The dress and adornment of the women was graceful. From the waist down they usually wear two very soft pieces of buckskin, the edges of which are cut into fringes and ornamented with strings of beads, snail shells and others of various colors which give a very pretty effect. One of these skins is worn in front and the other behind. From the waist up they wear what is called a *tapalo* of fox, otter, squirrel or rabbit fur, oblong in shape and very comfortable. Tying the opposite corners together, they thrust their head and one arm through the aperture . . . They adorn their heads tastefully with necklaces and earrings. Their hair is worn in bangs cut short and combed forward . . . they trim it daily by singeing it hair by hair with a piece of pine bark so that no hair protrudes. They wear side locks but the rest of the hair is worn loose, slicked down on top . . . Their headdress or coiffure gives the women a neat and graceful appearance and makes them less horribly ugly than the rest of the gentile women, giving them some attraction for the Spaniards.

He also reported that the Indians painted their bodies with red ochre, each *ranchería* having a distinctive pattern so that they could be recognized whenever they gathered for a dance or other function. The only instance of hats was recorded near San Luis Obispo. Fages (*op. cit.*, p. 49) wrote: "For an ornament and as a protection from the sun, they cover their heads with little woven trays or baskets, decorated with handsome patterns and shaped like the crown of a hat." Great numbers of necklace beads have been found, made of shell, bone, steatite, and other stones. Sometimes necklaces were made of eagle and bear claws.

Later archaeological work uncovered evidence of another form of skirt worn by the Indian women not noted by any of the diarists. It was a grass skirt reaching the knees, the tip of each blade of grass weighted with a dab of asphaltum (Rogers, 1929, p. 408).

As this manuscript was going through final revision, an article on the Cessac expedition was published in Paris with three excellent photographs of a Chumash Indian. These are shown here and in figure 62. These pictures will come as something of a shock to those accustomed to the smooth-chinned and hawk-nosed image of the American Indian. The features of this Indian are more Australoid than Mongoloid, and the beard is a feature often noted by the explorers. The diarists said that some of the men kept their beards plucked with clamshell tweezers—Father Ascensión called Santa Cruz Island the island of the bearded people.

31

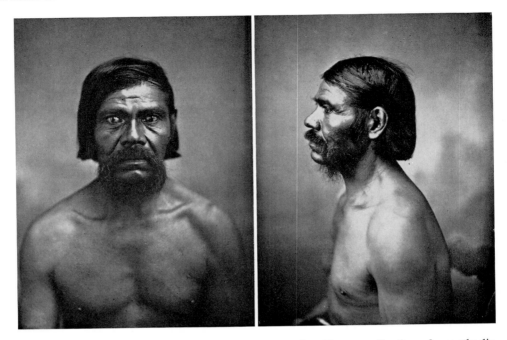

FIGURE 21.   A Samala Chumash from the Santa Ynez Valley. From a collection of recently discovered photographs taken by Léon de Cessac in 1878. (Collection Musée de l'Homme, Paris)

Villages and Population

The Chumash villages on the channel coast were usually built on high ground where a creek ran into the ocean. Thus they had fresh water and a quick launching spot for their canoes. Crespí (see Bolton, 1927, p. 158) describes his first look at a village:

> . . . we arrived at the shore where we saw a regular town, the most populous and best laid out of all we had seen on the journey up to the present time. It is situated on a tongue or point of land running out on the same beach . . .

On the islands, the settlements were chiefly on the high bluffs overlooking the sea and near the few springs and streams. In the mainland interior the villages occupied the benchland along streams or the *potreros*, high grasslands in the mountains. It is doubtful if all the villages or encampments were occupied the year round. There must have been seasonal movements for acorn and general seed gathering as well as hunting. In case of drought or an intermittent water supply, a breaking up into family groups and migrations to the permanent water in the headwater canyons must have occurred.

We have evidence that the major settlements were occupied over a long period of time by the same people. In 1542, Juan Paez, the Cabrillo diarist, wrote down the names of many of the towns (see Bolton, 1925, p. 26) and in mission times 250 years later, some of the names are recognizably the same.

Cabrillo	*Mission Records*	*Present Location*
Xuco	Succo	Rincón Point
Múgú	Múgú	Mugú Point
Misesopano	Misopsno	Carpintería
Coloc	Coloc	Toro Creek (near Carpintería)

It is difficult to arrive at an approximate figure for the Chumash population at the start of the mission era. The estimates of the explorers and early missionaries vary considerably, and these estimates are for the channel coast alone. Father Palou, in writing the Viceroy, gave an estimate of 20,000 along the coast but, as he was asking for funds, may have padded the figure. Crespí, a shrewd observer, thought there might be as many as 10,000 between Assumpta (Ventura) and Point Concepción.

There can be no doubt that the channel area had an amazingly dense population when the Spanish arrived. The first diarist, Juan Paez, records 41 pueblos between Assumpta and Point Concepción. There is a gap in his count of about 25 miles in this section which Paez simply says was thickly populated. On the island of Santa Cruz he noted eight pueblos; on San Miguel, two; and on Santa Rosa, three.

Two hundred and twenty-seven years later, Fages and Crespí took notes on 14 villages between Assumpta and Point Concepción and recorded the number of houses and Indians. The pueblo on Mescaltitlán Island had the largest number of houses (100) and over 800 Indians. In the estuary area including the island, Fages estimated about 2,000. The smallest settlement was near Point Concepción and numbered 24 houses and 200 people. Above Point Concepción, the channel ends, and to the north the Spanish saw only small, poor villages and no canoes, though Menzies in 1793 saw a planked canoe at Estero Bay near San Luis Obispo. It was probably for limited offshore work, as the northern coast, unprotected by the island chain, is beaten by too heavy a surf to permit the use of the light, plank canoe.

A summary of the estimates of Fages and Crespí gives a total of 5,800 for the coastal settlements and an average of eight people for each house. None of the explorers went inland, but Paez wrote, "They say that in the interior, there are many pueblos and abundant food" (Bolton, 1925, p. 27). In 1804, Father Tápis made a survey of the Santa Ynez Valley just before the founding of the Santa Inés mission and recorded 14 rancherías (Indian settlements) ranging in number of houses from 8 to 50 with a total population of 1,008.

The baptismal records at the Santa Barbara mission show 191 rancherías in the area and 23 on the islands that had furnished neophytes. In 1796, ten years after the mission founding, the army commander lists 19 rancherías and 1709 pagan Indians. The same baptismal records give us a final clue. Baptisms at San Luis Obispo mission, 2,909; La Purísima, 3,386; Santa Barbara, 4,686; Santa Inés, 1,631; Buenaventura, 3,924, for a total of 16,534 baptisms from 1772 to 1850.

There are no figures on the great inland valleys of the Cuyuma and the Carrizo and none for the immense mountainous area which must have supported   33 a considerable number of small bands. Kroeber has estimated a total Chumash population in 1770 at 10,000. This is certainly conservative.

Houses

The explorers all admired the large, well-made houses, and Martínez (see Simpson, 1961) has left a good description:

> These Indians live in communities and have a fixed domicile. They arrange their houses in groups. The houses are well constructed, round like an oven, spacious and fairly comfortable; light enters through a hole in the roof. Their beds are made on frames and they cover themselves with skins and shawls. The beds have divisions between them like the cabins of a ship, so that if many people sleep in one house, they do not see one another. In the middle of the floor they make a fire for cooking seeds, fish and other foods, for they eat everything boiled or roasted. Next to their houses they build smaller ones in which to store seeds, dried fish, sardines and other things against the winter when the cold, rain and roughness of the sea prevent foraging.

Fages (1937, p. 25) wrote: "... a reed mat serves as a mattress and four others as curtains forming a bedroom. Beneath the bedsteads are the beds of the little Indians, commodiously arranged." A padre (see Bolton, 1930, pp. 250–252) describes the house construction:

> Some of them have two or three holes like little windows. The frames of all of them consist of arched and very strong poles and the walls are of very thick grass interwoven. The door is a mat which swings toward the inside like a screen, and another toward the outside which they ordinarily bar with a whalebone or a stick.

FIGURE 22.
Chumash house, based on accounts by the explorers. About 18 feet in diameter.

Crespí wrote that some of the houses he entered were so large that as many as 60 families lived in one of them, and Paez mentioned houses on the islands that held 50 people. Another account speaks of houses 50 feet in diameter. There is no archaeological evidence to prove the existence of such gigantic structures. Rogers says that his investigations show houses from 12 to 20 feet in diameter. Olson excavated a house 16 feet 8 inches in diameter. The frame was of poles supported by four or five posts near the center. The door was formed by two whale ribs placed to form an arch. The roof was thatched with surf grass 2 to 3

34

inches thick. A rough circle of stones marked the fireplace in the center. The whole floor was covered with sand. There is ethnographic evidence that stools of whale vertebrae were often used and that houses were thatched with tule, carrizo grass, wild alfalfa, and fern.

FIGURE 23.   Interior of a California Indian house. (After Bartlett, 1854)

In every village there were one or more sweat houses or *temescals*, and Father Font took a good look at one (Bolton, 1930, pp. 250, 254):

> This is a hot, closed room for sweating, made somewhat subterranean and very firm with poles and earth, and having at the top, in the middle, an opening like a scuttle to afford air and to serve as a door through which they go down inside by a ladder consisting of straight poles set in the ground and joined together, one being shorter than the other. I peeped into a *temescal* and perceived a strong heat coming from it. In the middle of them, they make a fire. The Indians enter to perspire, seated all around and as soon as they perspire freely and wet the ground with their sweat, they run out and jump into the sea . . . They are accustomed to carry a sweat stick which is a long and somewhat sharp bone or similar thing with which they scrape the body when they are perspiring to remove the perspiration. They say that this is a good thing because by so doing they cease to be tired.

Longinos Martínez (see Simpson, 1961, p. 52) was shocked by the temescals and wrote:

35

This rite, which seems truly repugnant to our way of life, they perform daily, even in the severest weather . . . these people are so addicted to it that the missionary fathers, even in the missions, allow them to have sweat houses and ponds of cold water for the daily ablutions that they all perform because of their cleanliness and their fondness for soaping themselves at all hours.

FIGURE 24. California Indian sweat house. (After Forbes, 1839)

FIGURE 25. Sweat stick made from the lower jaw of a porpoise, used in the temescals to scrape off moisture. Length, 11½ inches. (Santa Barbara Museum of Natural History)

The bulb of the soap plant or amole and the crushed blossoms of the ceanothus were used to provide a lather. It makes a curious picture—the padres in their heavy, sweat-stiffened woolen robes, disapproving but tolerating the pagan practice of cleanliness. According to Father Maynard Geiger (1960, p. 9), only the men used the sweat houses, which served somewhat the function of a club, but an earlier observer states, "Men and women enter them twice a day . . ." (see Simpson, 1961, p. 52).

Kroeber (1925, pp. 810–811) wrote:

The Californian sweat house is an institution of daily, not occasional service. It is a habit, not a medicinal treatment; it enters into ceremony indirectly rather than specifically as a means of purification. It is the assembly of the men and often their sleeping quarters. It thus comes to fulfill many of the functions of a club . . . Women were never admitted except here and there on special ceremonial occasions . . .

36

Before a hunting trip, the hunters used the temescal to remove all human scent. The extremely close approach to game practiced by the Indians made this imperative.

Society

Political Organization

Of the village government, Fages (1937, pp. 32–33) wrote:

> In each of these villages . . . there is a captain . . . This chief has hardly any other function than that of the military command; they always choose the most conspicuous and intrepid one in the village. The position is for life and the incumbent enjoys an absolute, total independence in the government. Although in this district the captains commonly enjoy the privilege of taking two or three wives and putting them away at will, the ordinary men have only one and may abandon her only in the case of adultery.

Crespí adds that ". . . all the towns have three or four captains, one of whom is head chief" (see Bolton, 1927, p. 38). We have the word of Paez that women could head the village as well as men (Bolton, 1925, p. 29):

> The ruler of these pueblos is an old Indian woman, who came to the ships and slept two nights on the captain's ship as did many Indians. The pueblo of Ciucut appeared to be the capital of the rest, for they came there from other pueblos at the call of this ruler.

Paez may have been mistaken in thinking there was intervillage organization. All the eighteenth-century writers speak of separate village government. Each village had its own hunting and gathering preserve. The rights to these gathering areas were jealously guarded and any infringement might lead to war.

An early account states that the chief received tribute from his people in the form of food and shell money. He made the call to ceremonies, invited other villages to dances, and entertained visitors. He could grant permission for other villages to enter or to hunt and gather seeds on his territory and usually collected a part of their take as his fee. He alone could declare war. Indians interviewed by J. P. Harrington gave this additional information. Social standing was by blood and not by wealth, and the position of chief was hereditary. Both men and women could be chiefs and rule over a village or a group of villages. The chiefs kept the ceremonial regalia and had the privilege of owning pet eagles and eagle nests.

Birth

Fages (1937, p. 49) gives a good picture of a birth and must have watched the operation:

> When an Indian woman is in childbirth, she makes a small hole wherever she may be when labor begins, even though it may be in the open field; she digs out the soil and puts in a little hay or grass neatly arranged, warms the fire . . . and composes herself tranquilly to give birth. She removes from her child the envelope and adhesions bestowed by nature, strokes it, and deforms the cartilaginous part of the nose by flattening; then she goes without delay to bathe herself in cold water.

Fages describes the cradle-carrier as being carried on the mother's back, but Martínez disagrees (see Simpson, 1961, p. 56):

> As soon as the child is born, it is secured to a small hand ladder . . . somewhat longer than the child's body. A bed of soft fibers and bits of grass is made in the middle. The child is wrapped and then secured with rope . . . Where the shoulders of the child project, an arch is made of some woven stuff . . . forming a kind of niche which is adorned about the edges with shells and strings of beads . . . The mother attends to it and gives it the breast without picking it up, but goes to the place where the ladder stands . . . It is never carried on the mother's back but is dragged from one place to the other.

Marriage

With the exception of the chief, the Chumash men had only one wife. The wedding ceremony consisted simply of saying "You love me and I love you" (*ibid.*, p. 56). Adultery was the only excuse for dissolving a marriage and seems to have been rather popular. An Indian wishing to remarry could marry only a widow or widower. The observant Menzies (1924, pp. 324–325) noted that the Chumash women did not seem overly strait-laced:

"In their demeanor they appeared shy and bashful and are not, we believe, naturally given to meretricious practice, though we observed some of them act the art of coquettes with considerable address." That adultery was not tolerated in every Chumash area is indicated by a statement from an old Mugú Indian about 1880. Both parties to adultery were shot to death with arrows and their bodies burned (Bowers, 1897).

A new bride was purchased from her parents with presents. In 1815, Father Señán wrote: "When our neophyte youths intend to marry, they offer to the bride and her parents some beads, an otter skin, a blanket or some similar thing" (Englehardt, 1930, p. 34).

Taboos

In common with many primitive (and civilized) people, the Chumash had their taboos and superstitions. We have records of a few of them. One of the most unfortunate is recorded by Martínez (see Simpson, 1961, p. 56):

> In this region they have the notion that unless they have an abortion at their first pregnancy, or if the child does not die immediately, they will never conceive again. Hence they murder many babies with the efforts they make, the blows they give themselves, and the barbarous medicines they take in order to induce an abortion, so that some of the women die and others are badly injured.

38

At the San Buenaventura Mission, Father Señán (Englehardt, 1930, p. 34) wrote:

> The pagans especially the old men cling to many of their superstitions. For instance, a fisherman will not eat of the fish or of the venison, rabbits, hares, etc., which he caught, believing he will in that case catch no more. In order to win at a game of chance, he must fast for some days; and if he loses, imagines that the winner fasted more. The husband may not touch his wife until the child can stand alone on its feet, otherwise he shall have no more children. When the wife is delivered of a child, the husband must abstain from meat for some time, lest the child die.

Some additional taboos were that the name of a dead person could not be mentioned until the name was given to a child. It was taboo for a new mother to touch meat or grease for one month. A husband could not hunt or fish during his wife's menstruation.

Entertainment

In common with the rest of the North American Indians, the Chumash were fond of music and dancing. Father Crespí notes the entertainment pressed on the Spanish (see Bolton, 1927, p. 168):

> They . . . wished also to entertain us, and it was clear that there was rivalry and emulation among the towns to come out best in the presents and feasts in order to win our approbation. In the afternoon the chief men came from each town, one after the other adorned according to their usage, painted and loaded with plumage and some hollow reeds in their hands, to the movement and noise of which they kept time with their songs and the cadence of the dance, in such good time and in such unison that it produced real harmony. These dances lasted all the afternoon and it cost us much trouble to rid ourselves of the people. They were sent away, charged with emphatic signs not to come in the night and disturb us, but it was in vain, for as soon as night fell, they returned, playing on some pipes whose noise grated on our ears. It was feared that they might frighten the horses for which reason the commander went out to meet them with some officers and some soldiers. They gave them some beads and implored them to go, telling them that if they came again to interrupt our sleep, they would not be welcome and would be given an unfriendly reception.

The Chumash had no drums. The musical instruments were flutes of elder wood or bone, blown from the end, over the edge, the musical plucked bow, whistles of bone and cane and rattles of split wood, cocoons, seashells, turtle shells, and bunches of deer hoofs.

A flat area for dancing and ceremonials was an important part of each village. Fages (1937, p. 36) described a dance at such a spot.

FIGURE 26.   Bone whistles, originally joined like a Panpipe. Note asphaltum plugs and marks left by asphaltum-sealed cord lashing. Length, 7½ inches. (Santa Barbara Museum of Natural History)

The women go to them well painted, and dressed as has been described (with antelope hide skirt), carrying in both hands bundles of feathers of various colors. The men go entirely naked, but very much painted. Only two pairs from each sex are chosen to perform the dance, and two musicians who play their flutes. Nearly all the others who are present increase the noise with their rattles made of cane dried and split, at the same time singing, very displeasing to us . . .

FIGURE 27.   Dance of the Indians at mission San José, 1806. This shows the typical California body painting in red, black, and white. From *Bemerkungen auf einer Reise um die Welt in den Jahren 1803 bis 1807*, by G. H. von Langsdorff. (Bancroft Library)

Rogers in excavating sites has recorded several instances of finding the beaks of swordfish near the heads of male skeletons. In one instance, around the head lay a thick sheet of overlapping triangular ornaments made of iridescent abalone shell. Each piece was pierced as if for fastening to a skin or fabric. The sword and scaly headdress must have been very striking. Rogers thought that the man might have danced in the character of the swordfish, a much revered fish for its habit of driving the prized whale ashore. Elaborate feathered dance skirts were worn for certain ceremonial dances throughout southern California.

Feathers were used in many forms in the ceremonies. Feathered ornaments were held in the hands, and erect headdresses were made of magpie, crow, and roadrunner feathers. Feather quill bands, common throughout California, were

40

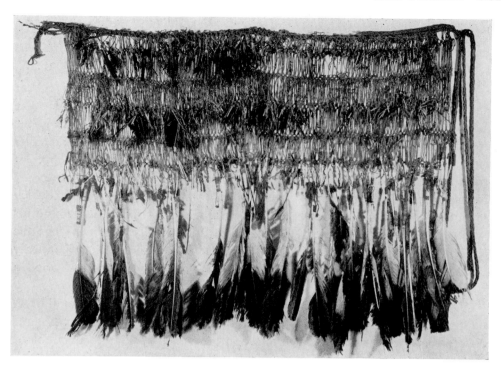

FIGURE 28. Ceremonial dance skirt from a cave in the Cuyama region. Eagle and crow feathers. Width, 33 inches. (Southwest Museum)

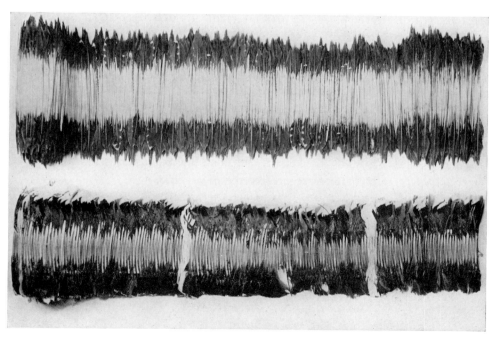

FIGURE 29. Feathered bands from cave cache. Upper, mainly flicker quill band; lower, pigeon or grouse (?) quill band. Length, 17 inches. (After Elsasser and Heizer, 1963)

41

of flicker feathers and occasionally of jay, pigeon, and pelican. The bands were worn on the forehead, down the back, as a bandolier or were hung on poles as a banner.

The Chumash undoubtedly played many games, and we have information on some of them. The game of shinny that most children have played in one form or another was originally an Indian game and was played by the Chumash. The usual playing field was about 400 yards long, and the goals two holes in the ground. Hardwood curved shinny sticks and a hardwood ball a little smaller than a tennis ball were used. In the mid 1840's, Alfred Robinson (1846, p. 94) saw the game of shinny being played at Santa Barbara before a large Indian crowd: "They played (in a large square) with a small ball of hard wood, which when hit, would bound with tremendous force without striking the ground for two or three hundred yards." He noted that immediately after the game the players retired to the sweat house. In addition, the Chumash undoubtedly played some form of soccer where the bare foot propelled a stone or wooden ball.

They also played some variation of the pole and hoop game. A small hoop made of tied rushes or bark was rolled along the ground, and the contestants tried to throw a long pole through the rolling hoop. They were great gamblers, and a favorite game was the old one of hiding a stick behind the back and having the opponent guess which hand held the stick. There was much pantomine and grimacing to help trick or confuse the other party. A game played mostly by women was the dice game. The dice were snail or walnut shells filled with asphaltum. Latta has described a similar game played by the Yokuts. It was played by four women, two pairs of partners. Halves of walnut shell were used, filled with asphaltum into which were pressed small bits of abalone shell to number the dice from one to eight. These eight dice were cast onto a large flat woven tray. Four combinations were used in scoring. Three flat sides up, one point; two flat sides up, one point; all flat sides up or down, five points; one flat side up, player lost a point and the dice went to the other side. A set of what may be gaming sticks has recently been found in a cave shelter. There are eight sticks of split elderwood, seven inches long and pointed at one end. They show much use and were probably dropped in a bunch for an odd-or-even game or to see whether the flat or round side came uppermost. Such a game was known to the Yokuts and was played and scored like the dice game.

Warfare

The Spanish found the Chumash gentle and friendly. Compared to the savage Plains Indians, they were not a particularly warlike people but there is evidence of a good deal of intervillage fighting and possibly some intertribal warfare. Fages (1937, p. 48) wrote that ". . . they are very warlike among themselves, living in almost incessant war, village against village." Near San Luis Obispo he noted (*ibid.*, p. 48):

> The men do not often sleep in their houses at night; but carrying with them their arms, bow and quiver, they are accustomed to congregate in numbers in great subterranean caves where they pass the nights in sheer terror; (if they stayed at home) they might be surprised in their bed by the enemy whilst defenseless on account of the presence of their wives and children.

About three miles west of Carpintería, a padre saw the ruins of a village (Bolton, 1927, p. 164):

> The heathen told us that about three months ago, the Sierra Indians had come down to fight and had killed all the people; two leagues and a half from our starting place we found the ruins of another village which had suffered the same disaster.

These may have been mountain Indians on raids against the channel villages in reprisal for some invasion of territorial rights. Excavations along the channel have turned up great numbers of skeletons with arrow and spear points imbedded in the bones and many with crushed skulls. It was a prestige factor to be a successful warrior, and Buchón, chief of a village near the present town of Pismo Beach, was celebrated ". . . for his valor and for the damage which he had done with his wars," according to Father Font (Bolton, 1930, p. 268).

Some idea of how war was waged was obtained by early investigators who interviewed surviving Indians years ago. The cause for a war could be infringement on a hunting or seed-gathering preserve, the refusal of a chief to accept an invitation to a dance or a feast, or the avenging of witchcraft. Kroeber states that warfare in California was carried on only for revenge, never for plunder. There is an account by a Mugú Chumash that a Tejón woman married a Mugú man and came to live on the coast. She was unfaithful to him and was killed according to the Mugú custom by being shot to death with arrows and her body burned. About four hundred Tejón Indians came over the mountains to avenge the death of the woman, and in the battle over seventy were killed. The Mugú Chumash, according to this source (Bowers, 1897), did not take scalps but cut off the right hand of the slain warriors.

The method of declaring formal war, as opposed to a surprise raid, was for the aggrieved party to send a messenger inviting a meeting at a certain place. Here both war parties met, throwing feathers in the air and crying "*ya ya ya ya*" for some time with increasing tempo, ending with a rousing "Wu-Kap-pee!" An Indian from one side then stepped forward and fired a series of arrows at the other side, whose warriors dodged the arrows. Then one from the opposite side shot off a quiverful. Three were killed in one such comic opera encounter between Santa Barbara and Rincón. Charmstones were sometimes worn during wars—it was believed that biting the stone made the warrior invisible.

Bancroft has written an account of precisely this same kind of formal war in northern California, complete with heralds to issue the challenges. An engaging detail is that each side would send boys to the opposing side between flights of arrows to pick up arrows and bring them back.

43

FIGURE 30. Flint spear point. Length, 4¼ inches. (Santa Barbara Museum of Natural History)

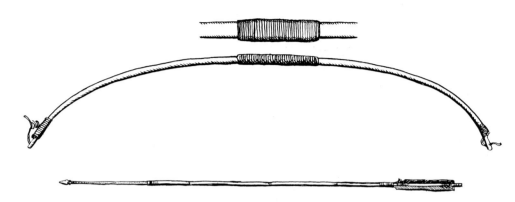

FIGURE 31. The Vancouver bow and a cane arrow from a cave in the Santa Barbara area. Length of arrow, 32 inches; bow, 40 inches. (Arrow, Santa Barbara Museum of Natural History; bow, British Museum)

The weapons were bow and arrows, war clubs, spears made of wood or wood with stone fitted to the head, and heavy flint knives hafted with wood.

Burial

The Chumash buried their dead in regular burying grounds in or near the village. Father Crespí wrote that ". . . one (cemetery) is for the men and the other for the women" (Bolton, 1927, p. 171).

In the earlier Chumash period, bodies were placed with the head toward the west, face down and roped in a flexed position. Since this was the position in which man enters the world, it was fitting that he should depart in the same manner. At a later period, re-burial was a usual practice, bodies being moved to make room for new ones. With the dead, offerings of bowls, beads, weapons, and charmstones were included. In many graves there was evidence that the wealth of artifacts placed with the body had been deliberately broken at the time of burial. One burial revealed a fine steatite olla that had been shattered into over a hundred pieces and then placed over the body.

The indispensable Lieutenant Fages (1937, pp. 33–34) has left an excellent description of the burial ceremony:

> When any Indian dies, they carry the body to the adoratory, or place near the village dedicated to their idols. There they celebrate the mortuary ceremony, and watch all the following night, some of them gathered about a huge fire until daybreak; then come all the rest (men and women) and four of them begin the ceremony in this wise. One Indian smoking tobacco in a large stone pipe, goes first; he is followed by the other three, all passing thrice around the body; but each time he passes the head, his companions lift the skin with which it is covered, that the priest may blow upon it three mouthfuls of smoke. On arriving at the

feet, they all four together stop to sing I know not what manner of laudation. Then come the near and remote relatives of the deceased, each one giving the chief celebrant a string of beads, something over a span in length. Then immediately there is raised a sorrowful outcry and lamentation from all the mourners. When this sort of solemn response is ended, the four ministers take up the body, and all the Indians follow them singing to the cemetery which they have prepared for the purpose, where it is given sepulture; with the body are buried some little things made by the deceased person himself; some other objects are deposited round about the spot where the body rests and over it, thrust into the earth is raised a spear or very long rod, painted in various colors. At the foot of this rod are left a few relics, which naturally represent the ability and kind of occupation which the man had while he was living. If the deceased is a woman, they leave strung on the rod some of the boxes and baskets which she was accustomed to weave.

The blowing of the smoke on the corpse and then to the four winds symbolized the release of the spirit. According to Kroeber, one man carried the body and made the grave. The widow wore some of her husband's hair on her head and observed food restrictions for a year. In some villages the grave was fired until the soil turned red and the body was placed on a bed of ashes. In other villages, the body was covered with a great slab of whalebone.

A most unusual female burial was excavated by Orr at Mescaltitlán Island in the Goleta slough. The body was found face down in typical flexed position on the scapula of a whale. The surface of the whalebone is inlaid with hundreds of beads and pieces of abalone shell. These are pressed into asphaltum, filling prepared grooves and depressions. A small sandstone bowl with inlaid rim lies against the left side of the skull, and two very large strings of beads are around each knee. This must have been the burial of a very important person or the work of a devoted craftsman and husband.

Small canoes of stone, bone, or wood have been found in the graves of infants. An old Chumash said that these were to help conduct the small soul across the vast space that separates this life from the great beyond. They may also have served as toys or dishes.

FIGURE 32.
Chumash smoking pipes of steatite. Left, pipe from dry cave still retains band of fiber around top. Length, including bone mouthpiece, 7 inches. Right, length, 6¾ inches. (Left, Santa Barbara Museum of Natural History; right, after Putnam, 1879)

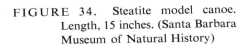

FIGURE 33. Wooden model canoe. These and the stone model canoes probably served as toys and eating vessels. Length, 6¾ inches. (After Putnam, 1879)

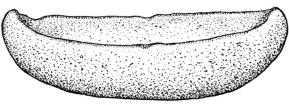

FIGURE 34. Steatite model canoe. Length, 15 inches. (Santa Barbara Museum of Natural History)

Social Attitudes

The Chumash attitude toward sexual aberration was highly civilized. It is commented on by nearly all the diarists. The naïve Crespí wrote (see Bolton, 1927, p. 171): "In this village as well as others in the channel, we have seen the heathen men wearing the dress of the women with buckskin petticoats, very well tanned and clean. We have not been able to understand what it means nor what the purpose is . . ."

Fages, the soldier (1937, p. 33), knew very well what it meant: "I have substantial evidence that those Indian men, who both here and farther inland, are observed in the dress and character of women—there being two or three in each village—pass as sodomites by profession . . . They are called joyas and are held in great esteem."

The practice of smoking was probably not confined to the shamans. The great number of pipes that have been found would indicate a more general use. The typical Chumash pipe was simply a tapering tube of steatite, usually with a bird bone mouthpiece, necessitating a tilted-back head position with a strong possibility of ashes in the eye. The tobacco was one of the varieties of *Nicotiana* and very strong. According to Father Tápis, "These neophytes . . . use a confection of wild tobacco and lime, which when it is chewed, strengthens them, as they say, but if they go to excess it intoxicates them . . ." (Englehardt, 1932a, p. 18). This was a paste called *perpibate*, made of tobacco and ground shells. The naturalist Martínez (see Simpson, 1961, p. 55) wrote: ". . . the Mexican Indians used to make little balls of tobacco and ground sea shells in order to endure thirst and hunger for a long time; these they place under their tongue and with the juices sustain themselves . . ."

Although the medicine man was called for any serious ailment, the Chumash had some knowledge of healing plants, roots, barks, and leaves. The powder of ivy was used for bear wounds. An aching part of the body was scarified. Purgatives and emetics were used.

46 The Chumash were not inclined to anger or cruelty, as were some of the Plains

Indians, and any form of punishment was rare. For theft, the culprit was brought before the chief and made to return the goods or something of equal value. Money was freely loaned without interest. Disputes between villagers were settled by the parties involved facing one another and exchanging blows with their sweat sticks until someone drew blood. The quarrel was then over.

Technology

The Chumash were superb craftsmen, and their work is found in many large museums today. Their cemeteries have yielded an abundance of artifacts of stone, shell, and bone. Some fine basketry has survived, most of it dating from mission times, and a few pieces have been recovered from cave shelters. Almost none of the perishable wooden artifacts have survived. In Font's diary (Bolton, 1930, p. 261), we find this entry:

> They make baskets of various shapes, and other things well formed, such as wooden trays and boxes, and things made of stone. Above all they make launches in which they navigate . . . Today in exchange for glass beads, the people obtained at the villages several baskets and stone cups very well shaped, and wooden trays of various forms and other curious pieces . . . they have nothing more than flints, and with them and their industry, they make their artifacts.

Stone

The finest objects made by the Chumash were of steatite or soapstone. Steatite has a low index of thermal expansion and will not crack when heated. It is also very soft and is easily carved and drilled. Its heat resistance made it ideal for cooking implements, smoking pipes, and arrow straighteners. The Chumash

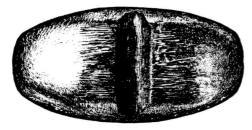

FIGURE 35.
Steatite arrow straightener. Length, 3½ inches. (After Putnam, 1879)

FIGURE 36.
Steatite tool or effigy. Length, 7¼ inches. (Santa Barbara Museum of Natural History)

47

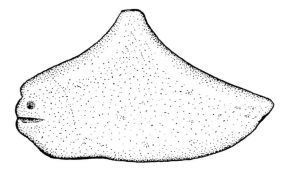

FIGURE 37.
Steatite whale effigy. Length, 8 inches. (Santa Barbara Museum of Natural History)

FIGURE 38.
Perforated steatite stone. Diameter, 4½ inches. (Robert Williams collection)

cane arrow was straightened by placing it in the groove of the heated stone and holding in the correct position until cool. The Chumash had no knowledge of pottery, and cooking was done with steatite ollas and *comals* or cooking stones, slightly concave rectangular slabs with a hole at one end to facilitate removal from the fire with a hooked stick. Small bowls to hold beads and prized possessions were commonly made of steatite. In addition, there were ladles, carved beads, effigies, often of the killer whale, and a number of curious artifacts that have baffled investigators for years. Great numbers of perforated stones of steatite and sandstone and looking rather like fossil doughnuts have been found, especially on the islands. They are from 2 to 4 inches in diameter with a hole between ½ inch and one inch. These have been variously described as weights for digging sticks, war club heads, and fishing sinkers. They have been found in fetish bundles with other typical shaman paraphernalia. The neighboring Yokuts used similar stones in rain-making ceremonies and as a game stone. Their game was exactly like that described to Bowers in the 1880's by an old Chumash: "Two people standing at a given distance from each other rolled the disk from one to the other while a third tried to catch it on a long pointed stick" (Bowers, 1897). This is a variation on the widespread Californian pole and hoop game. Bowers also recorded a number of such stones with wooden hafts fixed with asphaltum from a cave in the mountains of Los Angeles County. It is obvious these stones served various purposes at different times and places.

Another artifact, the use of which is unknown, is shaped roughly like a small hay baling hook with hand grip and sharply curved hook. This might have been used for some utilitarian purpose or may have been a ceremonial object, possibly representing a bird.

One of the most interesting artifacts is the charmstone, a cigar-shaped stone made of steatite, alabaster, schist, granite, and other rocks capable of taking a

48

fine finish. They vary in size from 1½ inches to nearly 18 inches. They are known to be ceremonial stones, and their use is described in the section on shamanism (pp. 66–68).

The steatite quarries nearest to the coastal Chumash country are on Santa Catalina Island, where, in a two square mile area, over three hundred quarry pits have been found. The inland Chumash traded for steatite with the San Joaquin Valley tribes (J. T. Davis, 1961). The softer and more micaceous variety of steatite was used for the cooking ollas and *comals*, while the denser type was made into pipes, ornaments, and ceremonial objects. The Indians, working the stone with flint scrapers, roughed out the exterior form of the olla while the base of the vessel was still attached to the rock. The mass was then broken loose, hollowed out, and highly finished on the outside. The Chumash made no pottery, though some of the neighboring Yokuts made much crude ware. Doubtless an unshakeable conservatism made them cling to their unwieldy and hard-to-get steatite ware.

Other implements were made of sandstone, a material available everywhere. Finely worked bowls up to six or seven quart capacity are common. The Chumash used the mortar and pestle for all their grinding. Some of the pestles are beautifully made, and some are nearly two feet long. The most interesting type of mortar is the basket mortar. A bottomless, funnel-shaped basket was cemented to the upper surface of a flat rock with asphaltum and served as a hopper while the meal was being pounded with a pestle. Rogers found a number of long,

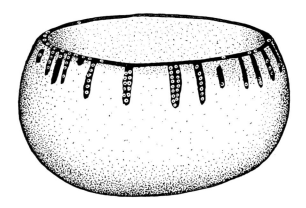

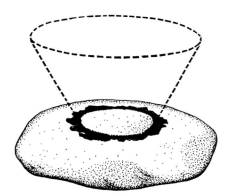

FIGURE 39. Large sandstone storage bowl with shell inlay decoration. Diameter, 22 inches. (Santa Barbara Museum of Natural History)

FIGURE 40. Basket mortar with hopper indicated by dotted line. Found at site V-1. Diameter of pounding surface, 5 inches. (Author's collection)

FIGURE 41. Sandstone pestle. Length, 15¼ inches. (After Putnam, 1879)

shallow stone containers with marks of carbon around the rims. These are invariably found inside houses and *temescals* and may be oil lamps.

Asphaltum was such an indispensable material to the Chumash that one might almost say that they had an asphaltum culture. It occurs in natural seeps in various parts of the Chumash area. They used it in every phase of their life. With it they calked their canoes, sealed the water baskets, attached the shell inlay to the bowls, and fastened arrow and spear points to the shaft. It was a complete adhesive and waterproofer, and was often used as a chewing gum. The asphaltum was kept in small cakes, and the method of application was by heating a long narrow stone and pressing it against the hardened cake in the manner of a soldering iron until the material flowed onto the surface to be worked.

The Chumash made very fine projectile points of flint or chert and occasionally of obsidian, which they obtained from the people to the east. The points are usually triangular with a notched base, or leaf-shaped with a rounded base (see figs. 30, 42, and 43). They also used flint for drills, scrapers, choppers, burins, and knives. Their burin was a specialized tool with a narrow chisel-like end, primarily for working bone or wood. These cutting tools were of great importance in working wood for canoes and utensils. The tools were made by percussion flaking, though the usual method of flint working was by pressure.

FIGURE 42.   Flint spearhead. Note the impression of cord and wooden shaft in remnant of asphaltum at base. Length, 11 inches. (Patrick Finnerty and Bryan Pearson collection)

FIGURE 43.
Chumash projectile point shapes.

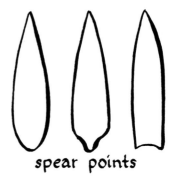

Drills were made by cementing a slender, sharp flint to a wooden spindle that was rotated between the palms of the hands. The countless thousands of tiny drilled shell beads that have been found show the efficiency of such drills. According to Kroeber (1925, p. 829), no California Indians knew of the more efficient pump drill until it was introduced by the Spanish.

The Chumash method of firemaking employed the same rotating spindle method. Fages (1937, p. 52) gives this description of the method:

These natives always carry their means of making fire in the shape of two small sticks attached to the net with which they are accustomed to gird themselves; one stick is like a spindle, and the other is oblong . . . in it there is a hole in the middle, in which the end of the other stick may be rotated. When they want to make a fire, they secure the square stick securely on the ground between the feet, and the round one, stuck into the hole, they rotate rapidly between the hands. It begins to smoke instantly and both sticks are burnt a little.

Wood

The finest technological achievement of these Indians was the splendid *tomol* or planked canoe. This canoe was unique in the New World. The only boat remotely like it was the dugout canoe with raised plank sides of the Araucanian Indians of southern Chile. There are excellent descriptions of the *tomols* from nearly all the Spanish diarists, who were unanimous in their praise. In 1602, the Viscaíno diary (see Bolton, 1925, p. 87) noted: ". . . a canoe came out to us with two Indian fishermen, who had a great quantity of fish, rowing so swiftly they seemed to fly. They came alongside without saying a word to us and went twice around us with such speed that it seemed impossible."

Nearly 200 years later, Font (see Bolton, 1930, pp. 252–253) wrote down the best description of the *tomol*:

FIGURE 44. Probably the only contemporary drawing of a Chumash canoe, with mission Santa Barbara and presidio in distance. (After Forbes, 1839)

51

> They are very carefully made of several planks which they work with no other tools but their shells and flints. They join them at the seams by sewing them with very strong thread which they have and fit the joints with pitch . . . Some of the launches are decorated with little shells and all are painted red with hematite. In shape they are like a little boat without ribs, ending in two points . . . In the middle there is a somewhat elevated plank laid across from side to side to serve as a seat and to preserve the convexity of the frame. Each launch is composed of some twenty long and narrow pieces. I measured one and found it to be thirty-six palms long and somewhat more than three palms high [the palm measurement varied from 3 to 4 inches]. In each launch . . . ordinarily not more than two Indians ride one in each end. They carry some poles about two varas [roughly six feet] which end in blades, these being the oars with which they row alternately . . . now on one side and now on the other of the launch.

The canoes ranged in size from about 12 feet to over 24 feet long with a beam of three to four feet. They were remarkably light (two men could carry an average-sized one) and seaworthy—ideal for riding through the surf and the swells between the mainland and the islands. In them the Indians made the round trip of over 100 miles to Catalina Island for steatite and ventured out to remote San Nicolás Island, 65 miles from the mainland. The wood could have been fir, redwood, pine, or some other of the conifers. Logs of these trees are sometimes stranded on the islands and along the shore. The Chumash word for pine is the same as that for canoe—*tomol*. For splitting the trees into planks, whalebone wedges were used instead of the usual deer antler of many California tribes. The stitching holes, as noted in fragments of canoes recovered from burial sites, were about two inches apart and an inch from the edge of the plank.

Daniel Hill, a New Englander who came to Santa Barbara in 1822 and married into a Spanish family, told of a craft unmentioned by the explorers (see Woodward, 1934, p. 119):

> They made canoes by digging out a solid trunk to contain four or five men, which were of a remarkably neat model and handsomely beveled, rounded off inside and out with hatchets made of stone and scrapers and knives formed of shells. They are about 30 feet long and 3 or 4 deep and wide. The stern and bow were shaped alike with a deep channel or groove for the anchor ropes to run through . . . Other canoes of similar size were made of stranded redwood trees after being split into planks.

Such a clumsy craft as the dugout might have had a limited value close to shore, but its use must have been rare, as we have only the one account of its existence.

In 1793, Captain George Vancouver visited Santa Barbara for supplies and water. Thanks to George Hewett, surgeon's mate on the *Discovery*, who wanted some curios to take home, a few wooden Chumash artifacts have been preserved. Four are now in the British Museum. The most interesting are a curious short *atlatl* or spear thrower and a harpoon with a heavy red painted shaft into which is set a slender foreshaft armed with a chert point and bone barb. The

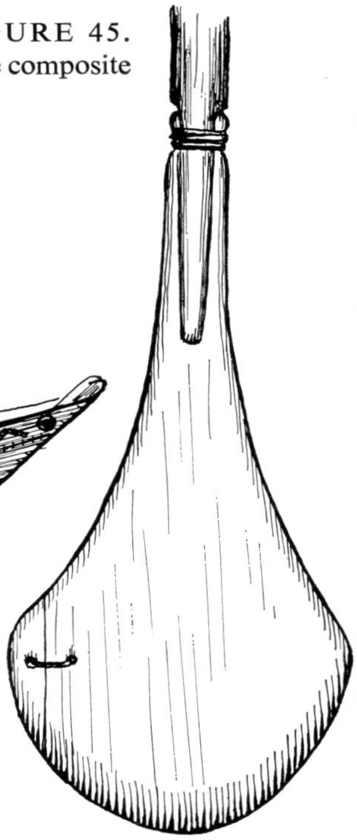

FIGURE 45.

The Chumash paddle taken by the Vancouver expedition. Extra lashings to secure composite construction missing. Width of blade, 6 inches. (After Dalton, 1897)

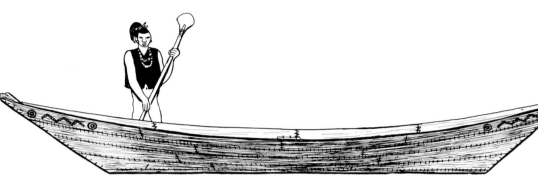

FIGURE 46. Chumash planked canoe. Length, 22 feet. Based on eye-witness accounts by Font (1775) and Menzies (1793).

other two artifacts are a section of one of the canoe paddles and a sinew-backed bow.

Recently a cache of Chumash arrows has been found in a rock shelter. The mainshaft is made of carrizo grass (*Phragmites*), a giant canelike grass; the fore-shaft is of wood. The arrows are finished with red-tailed hawk feathers and chert points, whipped on with sinew. The typical two-piece arrow in southern California has a mainshaft of *Phragmites*, but along the cool Santa Barbara coast, where the carrizo grass does not grow, the abundant and similar giant rye (*Elymus condensatus*) was probably substituted. Occasionally, the arrow was a single piece of wood sharpened at the fore end.

For a description of other wooden objects, we must refer to the explorers' journals. Fages wrote that the Indians made variously shaped plates from the roots of the oak and alder trees. Font spoke of well-formed trays and boxes. These boxes were made of small planks sewn together and sealed with asphaltum. Wooden ladles were used, and several have been preserved. The men carried in their hair a small knife made of a tongue-shaped flint fastened to a handle of straight polished wood inlaid with shell.

FIGURE 47. Flint knife set in shell- and asphaltum-decorated wooden handle, restored. Length, 8½ inches. (Santa Barbara Museum of Natural History)

Two superb Chumash wooden bowls were rediscovered recently by Dr. Robert F. Heizer in the Cessac collection in Paris. They are carved from oak, stained red, and highly polished.

53

FIGURE 48. Carved oak bowls collected in the Santa Ynez Valley in 1878 by Léon de Cessac. These are the only known surviving examples of the fine wood carving described in 1769 by Miguel Costanso "... *wooden plates and bowls of different forms and sizes made from one piece, so (skillfully) that not even those turned out on a lathe could be more successful.*" Left, 14 inches in diameter; right, 23 inches. (Collection Musée de l'Homme, Paris)

FIGURE 49. Flint burin. This is the type of tool used in shaping wooden objects like the Cessac bowls. Length, 2½ inches. (After Heizer and Kelley, 1962)

Basketry

Basketry was the most highly developed art of the California Indians, and those made by the Chumash were outstanding in workmanship and design. The Spaniards prized them highly and collected many as curios to be sent to relatives in Mexico, Peru, and Spain.

Baskets were the main household utensils and indispensible in the gathering of seeds, bulbs, and roots. Water was stored and carried in basketry bottles ingeniously waterproofed on the inside with asphaltum. (For a description of the waterproofing process, see Appendix A.) Seeds were winnowed by tossing in a basket and parched by shaking with hot pebbles in a shallow tray. Food was stored in large baskets, and loads were carried in pack baskets supported by a woven strap over the forehead. There are less than two hundred known Chumash baskets; a few have been found in cave caches, but most were collected in mission times and are in museums and private collections.

The Chumash basket weavers used both the coiling and twining techniques. For the coil foundations, they used the rush *Juncus textilis* in a three-stem bundle or, more rarely, a bundle of deer grass stems (*Epicampes rigens*). The wrapping is usually split *Juncus* stems in natural browns and straw or dyed black. For a whitish color, they used split, peeled sumac shoots (*Rhus trilobata*).

54   In the coiled ware there are basin-shaped baskets for food preparation, bur-

den baskets with flaring sides, large globular baskets for storage, and nearly flat circular trays for winnowing and parching. The finest workmanship is on small globular trinket baskets or necked, jar-shaped baskets. Flat, circular gambling trays and basketry caps have been found in mountain caves.

The twining method was employed for basketry water bottles, seed beaters, and coarsely woven basin-shaped baskets, probably strainers. The materials are whole *Juncus* stems and tule rush. There were other uses for basketry: cradles, hoppers for grinding mortars (figure 40), and bait baskets for fishing. Much use was made of sewn or twined tule mats.

FIGURE 50. Left, necked "treasure basket," diameter 8½ inches. Right, parching tray, diameter 13¾ inches. (Left, Southwest Museum; right, Chicago Museum of Natural History)

The designs are simple and invariably geometric. Almost every decorated basket has a horizontal band of decoration about an inch wide, spaced below the rim by about its own width. In addition, most baskets have rim ticks (five or six blocks of alternating black and light checks on the rim).

A detailed study of Chumash basketry was made by Dawson and Deetz in 1964.

FIGURE 51. Typical basketry designs from the Santa Barbara area. (Santa Barbara Museum of Natural History and James Deetz collection)

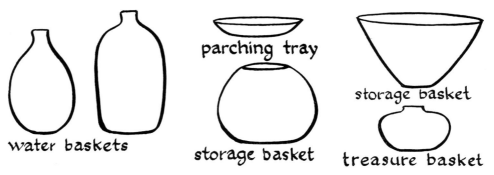

FIGURE 52. Some Chumash basketry shapes.

FIGURE 53. Asphaltum-lined water basket. Diameter, 11 inches. (Santa Barbara Museum of Natural History)

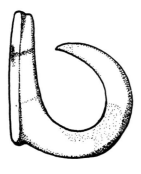

Shell and Bone

The most useful of all the shells available to the Chumash was the abalone, *Haliotis,* abundant along the channel. The shell was used whole as an eating dish after the row of siphon holes in the shell was plugged with asphaltum. In a few cases, these plugs were decorated with tiny perforated shell disks. The almost circular fishhooks were usually made from abalone shell, but sometimes the turban and mussel shells and bone or stone were used. The major use for this

FIGURE 54. Abalone shell fishhook. Hooks very similar to this were used in Tahiti. Length, 1½ inches. (After J. P. Harrington, 1928)

splendid shell was for decoration. It was lavishly inlaid on stone, bone, and wood. The surface to be decorated received a coating of asphalt into which was pressed the shell inlay. The beautiful iridescent inner surface of the abalone was often cut into perforated spangles of various sizes and shapes. These have retained their luster to the present time.

The keyhole limpet *Megathura* was used as a hair ornament. The univalve *Olivella* was a favorite bead material, being drilled and used entire or halved. The giant Pismo clam, *Tivela stultorum*, was used for beads and money. The clamshell disk money (about ¾ inch in diameter) was strung and traded by length of string. Strings as long as the circumference of palm and outstretched fingers were a basic money unit, and these units were often worn by the men

FIGURE 55.
Pismo clam shell money. The lines are incised and filled with asphaltum to bring out design. Diameter, ¾ inch. (Author's collection)

around their heads to be handy for gambling or trading. The Chumash were among the wealthiest of the California Indians, as their territory embraced the northern part of the Pismo clam range and furnished most of the supply of clamshell money for southern California. Slender drilled tubes of clamshell up to 3½ inches long were highly prized as money, and were sometimes worn in the pierced septum of the nose. According to Henshaw, the tiny holes in the longer tubes were drilled with sea lion whisker bristles.

The Chumash made a great many bone artifacts. They used bird bones and the bones of many mammals, especially deer, seal, and whale. Many pointed and polished bones are found that were almost certainly used as awls. Sweat sticks were made of bone, some with inlaid shell handles. A composite barbed hook was made with a bone barb tied to a stone shank. Bone was extensively used in the making of necklaces, especially for long tubular beads. Flutes and whistles were made of bone, the latter usually of deer tibia.

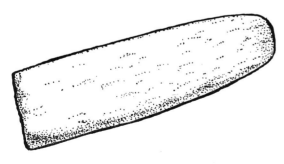

FIGURE 56. Whalebone wedge. Length, 5¼ inches. (Santa Barbara Museum of Natural History)

FIGURE 57. Composite steatite and bone fishhook. Length, 5¼ inches. (Santa Barbara Museum of Natural History)

57

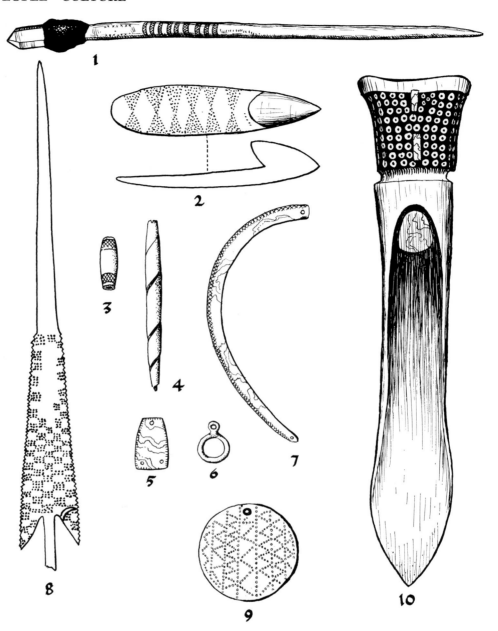

FIGURE 58. Chumash bone and shell artifacts. 1. Crystal-headed pin of mammal bone. 2. Possible atlatl tip of whale ivory. 3. *Tivela* tube. 4. Univalve shell columella. 5–7. *Haliotis* ornaments. 8. Ceremonial spear head (swordfish beak). 9. *Tivela* disk. 10. Ceremonial wand or dagger (grizzly bear femur). No. 8, 18 inches; no. 1, 8 inches; remainder to scale of latter. (Nos. 2 and 10 after Gifford, 1940; others after Gifford, 1947)

Whalebone was used for many things. The wedges to split wooden planks were of whalebone, as were the bars to prize loose the abalones. In the interior of the country, the wedges were of deer antler.

Shell and bone objects were formed by means of an abrading stone, a sandstone boulder against which the material was rubbed to grind it down to the proper shape. These rocks are readily identified by the many deep grooves worn in them.

Cordage

These Indians made excellent string and rope from a variety of raw materials. Perhaps the most widely used material was yucca, which made a coarse but very strong cord. For a more pliable string, Indian hemp *Apocynum*, nettle *Urtica*, or milkweed *Asclepias* was employed.

The raw material was stripped from the plants, dried and rolled on stones to separate the fibers. It was then rolled on the thigh into a single piece and twisted clockwise with another strand to form the basic two-ply cord. For stronger cord, three two-ply pieces would be combined counterclockwise in exactly the same manner as commercial rope today.

The heavier cordage was used for such things as anchor ropes for the canoes or harpoon line. The lighter material served many purposes such as fish nets, carrying bags, bowstrings and all kinds of tying and securing.

Language

> *Dios cascoco upalequen* Alaipai *quia-enicho opte; paquinini juch quique etchuet cataug itimi tiup caneche Alaipai. Ulamugo ila ulalisagua piquiyup guinsceaniyup uqui amog canequi que quisagiu sucutanajun utiagmayiup oyup quie uti leg uleypo stequiyup il auteyup. Amen.*

This is the Lord's Prayer as translated into Chumash by the Franciscans at the Santa Barbara Mission. The padres learned only enough of the language to make the initial contacts with the Indians or until the neophytes could be taught Spanish. Later much of the language was obtained from living Indians by investigators like Loew, Gatschet, Pinart, Yates, Henshaw, Kroeber, and J. P. Harrington. H. W. Henshaw compiled a large Chumash vocabulary in 1884; the most complete section, from the San Buenaventura area, was obtained from an educated halfbreed, Juan Pico. Pico also furnished Henshaw with a long discourse on American Revolutionary history, of which the following is a sample:

> *Washington ca canaay wot y jaaj si cal y nutiwatesh lo si ajutekuel ca si utiwate si ial ishmock sha aphaneshmu.* Washington was the first President of the United States elected under the Constitution.

The spoken language is said to have contained many harsh gutterals and clicking noises made with the tongue. J. W. Powell (1891) was the first to apply the word Chumashan to dialects spoken along the channel and in the San Luis Obispo area. This derives from the Chumash, the name of the Santa Rosa Islanders (phonetically *Tchumac*). Kroeber (1925) thought it came from the Indian name for Santa Cruz Island (*Mitc-tcu-mac*).

Chumash belongs to the Hokan linguistic superfamily, one of the six super-families of North America. In California the Hokan-speaking people are the Yuman, Chumash, Salinan, and Esselen of southern California, and the Washo, Pomo, Yana, Karok, and Shastan of northern California. In the Chumash territory, many dialects were spoken. Kroeber roughly divided the Chumash country into the areas in which each dialect was spoken. These are Obispeño, Purísimeño, Ynezeño, Barbareño, and Ventureño, the missionized districts; Island, Cuyama, and Emigdiano, the offshore and mountainous inland districts. About these dialects, Kroeber (1925, p. 552) says:

A rough classification of the known dialects is possible. That of San Luis Obispo, the most north-westerly, thrust into an angle between the Salinan and the sea, is the most divergent. Next in degree of specialization seems to be that of the islands. Santa Ynez and Santa Barbara are rather close. Ventura somewhat more different. San Emigdio seems to lean on Ventura.

Almost nothing is known of the dialect of the Cuyama area, the largest Chumash territory and the area containing by far the greatest number of pictographs.

The Chumash had a simple and efficient method of counting:

1. *pa-ka*   6. *yiti-ckomo*
2. *icko'mo*   7. *yiti-masex*
3. *mas-ex*   8. *mala'wa*
4. *cku'mu*   9. *tspa*
5. *yiti-paka*   10. *kel-co'mo*

11 to 19 were made by putting *na* before the 1 to 9 numbers. 20 is 2–10 or *icko mo-a-kel-co'mo*; 30 is 3–10 or *mas-ex-a-kel-co'mo*, and so on (Kroeber, 1910, p. 267). Here is a short list of Chumash words from over 200 collected by Dr. Oscar Loew at Kasua or Cieneguita near Santa Barbara in the 1870's (see Gatschet, 1879, pp. 424–464):

man	*oho-ikh*	grass	*twu-eg'e*
woman	*e'neke*	bear	*khus*
house	*a'p-h*	mosquito	*pu-u-u*
pine	*to-molgh*	rattlesnake	*khsab*
sun	*a'lish*	red	*ta-sen*
rain	*shtu'huigh*	white	*o-uokh*
water	*o*	black	*akhi'ma*
mountain	*mi-polomol*	good	*me-psuma'vish*
island	*shna-khala'mo*	bad	*piukh-pan*

There are many Chumash words still in use as place names in the Santa Barbara area. Such names as Cuyama, Piru, Hueneme, Ojai, Mugú, Cachuma, Sisquoc, Lompóc, Matilija, Nojoqui, Castaic, Malibu, and Sespe appear on the latest highway maps.

Religion and Shamanism

We know almost nothing of the Chumash religion. Of their traditions, beliefs, and ceremonies we get only the faintest, most provocative glimpses in the diaries of the explorers and the reports of the missionaries. In 1542, Cabrillo's diarist (see Bolton, 1925, p. 30) wrote:

> They have in their pueblos large plazas, and have an enclosure like a fence; and around the enclosure they have many blocks of stone set in the ground, and projecting three palms above it. Within the enclosures they have many timbers set up like thick masts. On these poles they have many paintings, and we thought that they worshipped them, because when they go dancing, they go dancing around in the enclosure.

Crespí says that he saw two such enclosures in a village, one for games and the other a ceremonial temple. On the same expedition, Fages (1937, pp. 32–33) wrote:

> Their idols are placed near the village, with some here and there about the fields, to protect they say, the seeds and crops. The idols are nothing but sticks, or stone figurines painted with colors and surmounted with plumage. Their ordinary height is three hands, and they place them in the cleanest, most highly embellished place they can find whither they go frequently to worship them . . .

Fages noted, "The god whom they adore and to whom they offer their seeds, fruits and all that they possess, is the sun" (*ibid.* p. 48). Later reports by the padres directly contradict this; one cannot help thinking that the Spanish, in their superficial observations, were doing a lot of guessing. A scrap of information that sounds authentic was gleaned by Bowers in the 1880's from a surviving Santa Rosa islander who was taken to the mainland in 1816 with the remnants of his people. He said that they were idolators and worshiped the sun, the sword-fish, and the raven (see Bowers, 1897).

The Franciscans, in common with missionaries the world over, were frankly hostile to the native religion and beliefs they were trying to supplant. In 1815, Father Señán of San Buenaventura Mission wrote, in answer to the government *Interrogatório* (see Englehardt, 1930, p. 35):

> Some old men pretending to be doctors, but being only graduated from the school of their own ignorance, simplicity and rudeness, tell a long series of ridiculous fables regarding the creation of the world and its government. The boys and the young folk take great delight in them and will even pay an old fellow to get him to recite his stories.

Further passages in the report (*ibid.*, pp. 34–35, 40) give a few clues about Chumash observances:

In the vicinity of their rancherias and on the mountain, they used to have some place which they kept very clean, swept and adorned with beautiful plumage put on poles. To these places they would go as to their sacred places. Here they would assemble in time of need and conduct a sort of pilgrimage. One of their number in the name of the rest who observed profound silence, would pray for rain offering an abundance of acorns, seeds, and wild fruits . . . They would catch fish and kill deer in order that no bear might catch them or the bite of a rattlesnake might not afflict them. They would pray also for health and other good things. At the end of the supplication, they would offer beads, acorns and various seeds in order that they might be regarded with favor by the invisible one . . . the author and giver of rain, seeds, fruits and other good things. It is preceded by a salutation which in our language means . . . "Grand Captain or Captain of Captains, behold us and hear what we say."

They imagine that after death, the souls are transferred to a place of delights where . . . there will be an abundance of fish and where they will have plenty to eat and will pass their time in play, dances and amusements. Thoughts of Last Judgment, Purgatory and Hell never entered their minds.

Father Olbés of the Santa Barbara Mission, in his report of 1813 (see Englehardt, 1923, p. 96) gives us the name of a Chumash deity:

When these neophytes were pagans, they worshipped neither the sun nor the moon, nor do they show any leaning in that direction. . . . they paid homage to a certain *Sup;* but we have no figure of this being nor can they say who he is. In honor of this *Sup* they throw on the roads and in various places, some seeds when they are gathering them, and also little feathers of birds, as if in gratitude and acknowledgement for the seeds, venison, birds, etc., which they have obtained in the course of the year.

This Sup is certainly the same as Achup or Chupu, worshiped by the Purísima Chumash. An early explorer noted that the Indians sprinkled seed on mats before the white men sat on them.

In 1801, a curious messianic movement occurred at the Santa Barbara mission after a severe epidemic of pneumonia and pleurisy that killed many Indians. An Indian woman neophyte in a trance had a vision in which Chupu appeared and told her that the pagan Indians would all die if they were baptized and that the same fate would befall the Christianized Indians if they did not pay tribute to Chupu and refused to wash their heads with a certain water. The news spread rapidly through the mission community, and all hurried to the house of the visionary to present beads and seeds and go through the ceremony of renouncing Christianity. The movement penetrated to all the Indian settlements of the channel before the Spanish had any news of it. Chupu had threatened death to any who would reveal the affair to the padres, but a neophyte broke down and told them. That the whole matter could have taken a dangerous turn for the Spaniards is indicated in a letter from Father Tápis to the governor (see Heizer, 1941, p. 129):

If the Indian woman had added, that in order to stop the epidemics, it was necessary to kill the missionaries and the soldiers of the guard . . . the natives would have believed it too, as they did the first part of the revelation. Who would have escaped and would have warned the Presidio though it is only half a league away?

The epidemic died down and the padres regained their control over the Indians, but the movement had been a demonstration of distrust and dissatisfaction with the new life. Something very like it may have been back of the serious uprisings of 1824. The Chupu ritual persisted among the missionized Indians and was observed by Daniel Hill in the 1820's (see Woodward, 1934, pp. 120–121):

> They often secretly build little temples of sticks and brush, on which they hang bits of rag, cloth and other paraphernalia, depositing on the inside, tobacco and other articles used by them as presents for the unseen spirits. This was the occasion of great wrath to the padres who never failed to chastise the idolators when detected.

We have one record that the Chumash practiced the *toloache* or Jimson weed cult. The governor reported in 1811 that the priests of Santa Inés claimed that their neophytes were using Jimson weed with accompanying ceremonies. In Latta's *Handbook of Yokuts Indians* (1949) there is a picture of a fine Jimson weed ceremonial bowl and pestle used in Tejón Canyon by Chumash who had migrated from near Carpintería.

FIGURE 59.
Very fine steatite bowl, probably for ceremonial purposes. Diameter, 9 inches. (Southwest Museum)

Toloache or *Datura meteloides* is a rank-smelling plant with a large white trumpet-shaped flower and is common throughout southern California. The Indians made a brew by grinding the dried roots of the plant and adding hot water. This liquor was a vision-producing narcotic and through its use there developed a cult, practiced in various forms by a number of southern California tribes. As we have no accounts of the Chumash ceremonial use, the puberty rite of the nearby South Yokuts will give some idea.

The boys to be initiated into manhood and tribal status fasted for about six days on thin acorn soup. During the fast, the old man in charge of the initiation told them of the creation of the world and their future life. When it was time to drink the Jimson liquor, the old man chanted as he offered the drinking basket to each boy. The boys were then taken to a secluded spot to sleep off their intoxication. The ceremony was supposed to give health, long life, general prosperity, and ability to dodge arrows. The immediate effects, of course, were visions and a fearful hangover. One boy participated in this ritual three times. The first time he was stupefied for six days; the second time, for three days; the third time, he did not sleep but walked around as if drunk. With some tribes the *toloache* was associated with elaborate mourning ceremonies for dead cult members. In the Canaliño cultural area, ritualistic figures of steatite have been found, many of them representing killer whales. According to Kroeber (1925, p. 938), these and also rock paintings may have been used in connection with the *toloache* cult.

FIGURE 60. Whale effigy of steatite from San Nicolás Island (sperm whale with killer whale dorsal fin). Length, 7 inches. (After Heizer, 1957)

FIGURE 61. Steatite effigy from San Nicolás Island. Length, 2⅛ inches. (After Cessac, 1882*b*)

Three bull-roarers have been found in dry caves in the Santa Barbara area. These are short, flat wooden staves with a drilled hole at one end. A string is attached through the hole, and when swung the stave makes a whirring, humming sound. These curious implements have been used by primitive man for many thousands of years, and there is at least one specimen of Mousterian age (Armstrong, 1936). Though ethnographically noted chiefly as a toy, there is little doubt that, before the break-up of the native religion by the missionaries, the Chumash bull-roarers were used ceremonially. Four were recovered from Bowers Cave in association with feathered bands, stone-tipped ceremonial wands, and Chumash-type baskets. Both caches are well within the region characterized by the ritual taking of *toloache*.

The main function of the shaman or medicine man in California was the curing of disease. Disease was thought to be caused by the presence in the body of a foreign object which was removed through the power of the shaman. Singing, dancing, and smoking tobacco often went along with the treatment. The power of the shaman could be benevolent or malevolent, and much disease was thought to be caused by hostile medicine men. These people claimed supernatural powers, and in California some became rather specialized. There were rain doctors, rattlesnake doctors, and bear doctors. The rain doctor controlled weather; the rattlesnake doctor cured or prevented snakebite; the bear doctor could turn himself into a grizzly bear and could then kill enemies. In the Cuyama area, I saw a cave with 49 bear tracks pecked into the rock. This might have been the work of a very potent bear doctor.

The shaman derived his power from a guardian spirit that appeared to him during a dream or trance. The spirit might be a dead person, perhaps a former shaman, or an animal. With the Yokuts, the guardian spirit of a bear doctor was a grizzly bear; of a rattlesnake doctor, the sun; of a rain doctor, usually some amulet.

FIGURE 62.
The same Samala Chumash shown in figure 21, wearing the ceremonial costume of a shaman. From a photograph by Léon de Cessac, 1878. (Collection, Musée de l'Homme, Paris)

The Santa Inés mission record (see Englehardt, 1932a, p. 16) gives a slightly biased account of a Chumash shaman at work:

> Generally the curative method employed in their illness consists of the deception which the sick undergo, whose authors are some Indians who in the pagan state are regarded as healers. These make the sick believe that their illness is caused by

65

some feather, claw of a leopard [mountain lion?], a chip, hairs, etc., which they have in the body. The patient, desirous of obtaining health, pays such frauds well, who in their arts and crafts pretend to extract the feather, etc., from the body, but in reality from their own hand. So the patient keeps his illness . . . Other healers have the method of extracting blood from the patient without any incision in the body. So the sick ignorantly believe, as the blood comes from the mouth of the same healer, who keeps it in a sore or wound, and when there is an occasion to suck blood . . . he takes into his mouth warm water, and pretending to suck or extract blood from the body of the patient, he takes it from his own mouth, mixed with water. This remedy is the *cura lo todo*, leaving always the sickness as it was . . .

Unhappily for the neophytes, the *cura lo todo* of the padres was equally inefficient in curing them of the Spanish diseases.

To suck the imaginary object from the patient, the doctor, called *Ach-ie* in Chumash, used a steatite tube. Another ceremonial stone employed by shamans was the perforated or doughnut-shaped stone. The Yokuts used such a stone to control weather (fig. 38).

FIGURE 63.   Steatite medicine tube. Used by doctors to conceal objects presumably sucked from the body of the sick person. Length, 10½ inches. (After Putnam, 1879)

A typical shaman's equipment or fetish bundle is described by Olson (1930, p. 19) from one found near Santa Barbara.

Of the contents of such bundles one example will suffice: painted fabric or basketry containing 2 perforated stones, 5 awl or spatula-like batons with quartz crystals set into the open ends, three loose quartz crystals, 2 steatite pipes, a small incised steatite dish, and a number of beads, pendants, curious shells, etc.

Rogers has found many objects presumably used by shamans, such as pecten rattles and various small effigies. In one undisturbed burial of a shaman, the bones of the hand still grasped a whistle made of four varying lengths of bone ranged side by side with the marks of the cord that lashed them together still visible in the asphaltum.

By far the most provocative tools in the shaman's bag of tricks were the charmstones. In the Chumash area, they are invariably made of a close-grained dense rock usually not native to the district, varying in size but averaging about six inches in length and carefully worked and polished. They are cigar-shaped and pointed at both ends. Rogers (1929) found two groups of these stones at a site he describes as a sacred compound or shrine. In each group were ten of the stones radiating out from a central round stone that rested in a small cuplike boulder. Many more charmstones were found buried in the stone-enclosed area. According to Yates (1889), a Chumash from the Santa Ynez Valley said that the medicine man would fast for a month and then take several cups of a drink called *toloache* before using the stones. Here is evidence of a connection between the *toloache* cult and the charmstones.

66

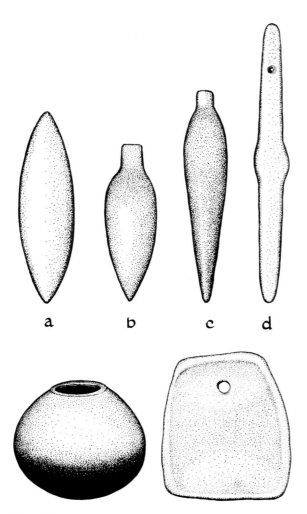

FIGURE 64. Top, charmstones. a. Santa Barbara County (Chumash). Length, 5¾ inches. b. Sonoma County (Pomo). Length, 4½ inches. c. Kern County (Yokuts). Length, 6½ inches. d. Sacramento County, amphibolite schist. Length, 7¼ inches. Lower left, steatite olla showing fire blackening. Diameter, 13½ inches. Lower right, steatite comal or cooking slab. Length, 9¾ inches. (a and lower figures, Santa Barbara Museum of Natural History; b, after Elsasser, 1955; c, Clarence Ruth collection; d, after Heizer, 1949a)

In 1889, Lorenzo Yates obtained a description of their use from a Chumash near Santa Barbara. They were very powerful sorcery stones, and the shaman arranged them in a circle of twenty, then shoved them violently together and sprinkled water over them. At Ventura the ceremony was similar but twelve stones were used. In the center of the circle was the stone *Tu-cait*, with chia seeds, breast down from a white goose, and red ochre spread over the whole. Around this a dance was held while three old men sang and shook rattles. The ritual was to cure the sick, bring rain, bring fish up the streams, and help in war.

Latta, a long-time student of the Yokuts Indians, gives a remarkably similar picture from that area. Great numbers of the charmstones have been found in 67 the San Joaquin Valley, and in ten authenticated instances they were arranged in circles of nine or ten. These stones differ from the Chumash type in that they are of a plumb-bob shape with a knob at one end and a point at the other. They were often hung on branches along streams to bring good fishing. Mrs. Mary J. Gates in a pamphlet, *Contributions to Local History* (1894), gives an account of the stones from northern Santa Clara County, based on conversation with the local Indians (probably Northern Yokuts). This description is extraordinarily like that given by Yates from Ventura nearly 300 miles away. The ritual must have been highly formalized over a large territory and indicates a religious affinity with central rather than southern California. Great numbers of charmstones have been taken from the bed of a dry lake in Sonoma County (see Elsasser, 1955, pp. 28–33). They have also been reported from Butte, Sacramento, Solano, and Napa counties. Heizer (1949) describes many charmstones from the Delta region of central California that have recently been dated at over 4,000 years. Both Heizer and Olson (1930) noted that most charmstones have been found in association with early burials, indicating a rather common usage. By the beginning of the historic period, charmstones were scarcer and seem to have been used solely by the shamans for ceremonial purposes.

To get any understanding of the religious beliefs of the Chumash, one needs to know something of the way the Indian's mind worked. Theodora Kroeber in her splendid book, *Ishi* (1961, p. 23), on the last of the Yahi Indians, gives a shrewd appraisal:

> The California Indian was . . . an introvert, reserved, contemplative, and philosophical. He lived at ease with the supernatural and the mystical which was pervasive in all aspects of life. He felt no need to differentiate mystical truth from directly evidential or "material" truth, or the supernatural from the natural; one was as manifest as the other within his system of values and perceptions and beliefs.

Food Gathering and Preparation

The most valuable plant in the Chumash economy was the oak. There are many varieties of oaks in the area, but the most abundant was the California live oak, *Quercus agrifolia*. The acorns were gathered in the fall and stored for use during the year. The method of preparation was probably very similar throughout California and, since we lack a Chumash description, the Yokuts method will be given.

To remove the hulls, the acorns were placed pointed end down in the shallow hole of an anvil stone and tapped on the large end with a mano. The shelled nuts were then put into baskets to cure. When thoroughly dry, the acorns were ground into meal with mortar and pestle. The common mortar for this job in the Chumash and Yokuts areas was of wood and often with basket hopper attached. The ground meal was sifted and the larger particles reworked until the acorn meal was reduced to the consistency of coarse flour. A shallow basin was scooped in the sand and lined with leaves, and the flour was placed in it. Hot water was then poured over the flour a number of times until the bitter tannic acid was leached away. The meal was left to harden into a cake, which was then taken into the house for cooking. The Yokuts today still follow this ancient method. The raw acorn cake was often simply broken into pieces and eaten. A thick acorn soup was made by pulverizing the cake and boiling in a steatite vessel. Much of this cooked mush was allowed to harden and then eaten as bread. The Chumash leached out the tannic acid in a basket filter called a *chaleel*.

The two basic cooking implements were the olla for boiling and the *comal*, a flattish stone pan, like a griddle, for frying. Both of these were invariably made of the heat-resistant steatite. Food was often eaten raw, especially on the islands.

Pine nuts, especially of the piñon pine (*Pinus monophylla*), were a favorite food. The wild cherry (*Prunus ilicifolia*) was bruised in a mortar and boiled. A number of early writers speak of the natives eating *mescal*. This plant does not occur in this area and the plant referred to must be yucca. The young flower stalk was roasted with hot rocks covered with earth. The cattail *Typha* gave seeds and flour from the roots for the making of *pinole* (any gruel or paste of ground seeds). Berries, mushrooms, and cress were gathered in season to add variety to the diet. One of the most useful of plants was the amole or soap plant (*Chlorogalum pomeridianum*). The bulb was roasted and eaten, it furnished a soapy lather for use in the *temescal*, the outer husks of the bulb were bound together and frayed to make brushes, and the crushed plant was used as a fish poison. The berries of the laurel (*Umbellularia californica*) were roasted.

A particularly valuable plant was chia sage (*Salvia columbariae*), a low-growing plant with a very oily seed that was made into flour. Water and sugar were added to make a highly nutritious food. Chia was also used medicinally. Sugar was obtained from the sweet wax covering of the sugarbush (*Rhus ovata*). An unusual source of sugar was honeydew (minute sweet droppings of such sucking insects as aphids, scales, and whiteflies). In the Chumash country, the insect was the aphid (*Hylopterus aundinis*) that swarms on its summer host, the carrizo grass (*Phragmites communis*) in great numbers, sucking the sap and excreting honeydew on the stems and leaves where it crystallizes. The canes were cut in the fall before the first rains, and dried and threshed to remove the droplets of honeydew. These were then gathered and pressed into balls or cakes resembling maple sugar. Salt was obtained by trade with the Yokuts, who collected the salty incrustations on a variety of salt grass.

There were many seeds in the food economy of the Chumash. Most of these were gathered with the aid of a seedbeater. This was a woven fan-shaped scoop with which the women would beat the seeds of grasses and other plants into a wide-mouthed basket held under the other arm.

For hunting, the Chumash had a variety of weapons. The most important, of course, was the bow and arrow. An early writer comments on the incredible number of arrow points being made all the time, and the number of points still   69 being found today bears this out. The single example of a spear thrower, brought back by the Vancouver expedition, may have been traded from some other area, as no early accounts mention its use. The California mule deer were plentiful throughout the territory and were hunted for food and skins. As an aid in deer hunting, the Chumash used the usual deer head disguise and are reported to have been able to run down deer on foot. Small game was taken with the spring-pole snare and various deadfalls. The sling was used as well as the curved throwing stick. In some areas, the brush was fired to drive rabbits into the open, where they were killed with throwing sticks. Bear cubs were trapped and fattened for eating, though the formidable adult grizzly must have been left strictly alone except by the very brave or foolhardy. Animal remains in the shell mounds include sea otter, sea lion, whale, porpoise, deer, coyote, fox, and many smaller animals. Whale, when washed or driven ashore, were eaten, and the great number of whale bones in the villages indicate that many came ashore. Seals and other marine animals were harpooned or killed with clubs. Many birds and bird eggs were eaten. The Indians were very fond of ducks, geese, quail, and the migratory doves and band-tailed pigeons. These were shot with bow and arrow and trapped or snared.

Mollusks of many kinds were eaten the year round (except the seasonally toxic mussel) by the channel Chumash. The enormous shell mounds or middens —some over twenty feet deep—mark the ancient villages on the islands and mainland. A quantitative analysis of shell material at a recently excavated Chumash house site at Morro Bay shows that the following four varieties make up the bulk of the midden: barnacle (*Balanus*), horse clam (*Schizothaerus*), Washington clam (*Saxidomus*), and California mussel (*Mytilus*). The big Pismo clam and the abalone, both abundant in the region, are conspicuous by their absence. Their shells were in great demand for money and ornaments and not likely to be thrown out with the refuse.

The Santa Barbara channel provided an inexhaustible supply of fish, from anchovies to the largest game fish. Whenever the channel was calm enough for navigation, the canoes would be launched through the surf and head for the fishing grounds. The larger fish were harpooned; the smaller ones were caught in dip nets and seines of twisted yucca and other vegetable fiber. Fages (1937, p. 51) describes the method of "chumming": "For catching sardines they use large baskets into which they throw the bait which these fish like, which is ground-up leaves of the cactus, so that they come in great numbers; the Indians then make their cast and catch great numbers of the sardines." A favorite bait was the mussel. The fishing lines were also made of plant fiber, and two types of hooks were used—one, an almost round hook made from the central part of the abalone shell (fig. 54), and the other, a more conventional hook with a wood or stone shank and a pointed bone barb lashed on at an angle (fig. 57). The abalone hook, almost identical with the Tahitian type, was designed to be swallowed by the fish. Many of these are recovered with fish bones in the middens.

The fish were eaten raw, roasted, or in a dried form, though most of the diarists indicated that roasting was the usual method. Along the mainland, the

70

creeks and rivers had a winter run of the large steelhead trout, which were taken by spearing. The mountain streams had a smaller land-locked variety of the same trout. These were netted or poisoned, possibly by the soap plant (*Chorogalum*) or turkey mullein (*Eremocarpus setigerus*), known to the Spanish as *yerba del pescado*. In addition, the Chumash, like most California Indians, would eat roasted grasshoppers when they were abundant.

Due to the great numbers of smaller food fish like sardines and anchovies, the channel supports large seasonal populations of barracuda, yellowtail, bonito, swordfish, mackerel, halibut, and tuna. Along the shore are perch and corbina, and the reefs swarm with bass and many kinds of rockfish. In the years when cold currents enter the channel, king salmon come as far south as Carpintería.

Intertribal Relationships

The Chumash shared many cultural traits with the people in adjoining territory. To the north were the Hokan-speaking Salinans. These Indians were not nearly as numerous as the Chumash; Kroeber estimated them at around 2,000 in 1770. They occupied a territory from the headwaters of the Salinas River north to Santa Lucia Peak in Monterey County, and from the sea to the crest of the Coast Range. In their midst, the missions of San Antonio and San Miguel were established, and in 1925 there were about 40 mixed bloods left.

To the northeast were the Yokuts of the Penutian linguistic group. They occupied the entire San Joaquin Valley and the foothills of the Sierra Nevada. The Yokuts were the largest Indian group in California, estimated at 18,000 in 1770. Far removed from mission influence, they were decimated by the predatory white settlers and, when confined to reservations, died of the white man's diseases. In 1910, the Yokuts were reduced to about 600, or 3% of their pre-white figure. To the east and southeast of the Yokuts were the Tubatulabal of the Kern River and the Kitanemuk of Tejón Canyon and the Tehachapi Mountains. These were small tribes of not more than 1,000 each, and in 1910 there were still a few hundred survivors.

To the east on the upper Santa Clara River was a small Shoshonean-speaking tribe, the Alliklik. Absorbed by the San Fernando and San Buenaventura missions, they vanished.

To the southeast were the Shoshonean Gabrieliño with a 1770 population of 5,000. The Gabrieleño shared many cultural traits with the Chumash, including the use of steatite cooking vessels and planked canoes. Late writers (Harrington and Rozaire, 1958, and B. E. Johnston, 1962) have lumped the two cultures as Canaliño. Their territory covered present-day Los Angeles and Orange counties, and the islands of Santa Catalina, San Clemente, and San Nicolás. The missions of San Fernando and San Gabriel were built by these Indians for the Franciscans. Today the Gabrieliño are all gone.

By a study of the objects that are foreign to the region but found in village 71

a Chumash
b Yokuts
c Salinan
d Alliklik
e Fernandeño
f Gabrielino

FIGURE 65. The Chumash and their neighbors. The three large islands southwest of the Gabrieliño area (f), starting clockwise from the closest inshore, are Santa Catalina, San Clemente,
and San Nicolás, all occupied by Gabrieliño Indians. The tiny island is Santa Barbara Island.

sites or recorded by early travelers, archaeologists are able to reconstruct the
probable trading patterns with adjoining tribes.

According to Davis (1961), the Chumash supplied the Salinans with steatite
and wooden vessels and beads. They traded white pigment, shell beads, Pismo
clam, abalone, olivella, limpet, and cowrie shells, and dried sea urchin and star-
fish to the Yokuts for black pigment, antelope and elk skins, obsidian, salt,
steatite, beads, seeds, herbs, and vegetables. They supplied the Tubatulabal with
asphaltum, shell ornaments, steatite, and fish in exchange for piñon nuts. The
mainland Chumash traded seeds, acorns, and bows and arrows with the island
Chumash for chipped stone implements, fishbone beads, baskets, and basaltic
rock. The Kitanemuk obtained wooden and shell-inlaid vessels from the Chu-

72

mash. From the quarries of the Gabrieliño on Santa Catalina Island, the Chumash acquired the all-important steatite, though the Yokuts afforded a much easier source for the inland Chumash. As an example of long-range trade, Font wrote that the Indians had woven cotton blankets from the southwest (see Bolton, 1930, p. 25).

A Yokuts Indian woman, Yoimut, born in 1855, gave this account of a Yokuts expedition to trade with the coast Indians (Latta, 1949, pp. 274–275). The trading point was somewhere in present southern San Luis Obispo County, and the coast Indians were Chumash or Salinans.

> The bead and seashell traders from the coast met the Tachi traders at Poso Chana. The Tachi and the other Indians would not let the people from the west come right up to the lake. They were afraid they would learn how to get things without trading.
>
> The people who wanted to trade carried their things in baskets on their backs. They had to have their *Teah* (chief) with them. When they came up to trade they marched up in a straight line from each side. The *Teah* was in front.
>
> When the two parties got close to each other they all took hold of the basket straps at the sides of their heads and swung from side to side, singing:
>
> *Ho-hoo-hoo Yoo-nah*
> (sung five times)
> *Hah-ha*
>
> *He-ke-mah* was the name of that song. That was the name of the trade too.
>
> When the song was done each took his basket down and spread his things on the ground in front of him. The rows of things were about ten feet apart. Then the trade started. The *Teahs* did all the talking for the people. They talked to each other and agreed how much each could have. It was all done by rules. *Kahnte* told me that his people used to trade off fish, *kots* (obsidian), salt grass, salt and some seeds. Sometimes they traded *kuts* (soapstone) beads. They brought back shell beads and sea shells. . . .

There is evidence that the Mojaves of the Colorado River frequently made trips to the coastal Chumash country, a journey of nearly four hundred miles. These warlike, primitive agriculturists were great travelers and probably carried the news of the Coronado expedition to the coast.

Father Señán reported an incident at the San Buenaventura mission in May, 1819. A small party of Mojaves arrived at the mission and, in a confusing encounter with the soldiers, ten Mojaves, two soldiers, and one neophyte were killed. A letter exists (see Simpson, 1962), from Señán to Captain de la Guerra, begging him not to "display the heads of the slain gentiles as usual in various places," as it might lead to trouble with the local Indians. A few days later he again wrote De la Guerra (Simpson, pp. 124-126):

> A recent letter from Father Vicente tells me that the Amajabas [Mojaves] visited the rancho San Francisco Xavier and that they were quiet and peaceful during their stay. When questioned about their future movements, they said they were going to San Buenaventura to gather abalones and sell some of the produce of their country. I feel their behavior here will be equally good if their enmity is not aroused. May this be God's will!

73

CHAPTER FOUR

The Paintings

The Chumash, according to the explorers, made lavish use of color. They painted their faces and their bodies, their spears and bows and arrows. The women stained their buckskin skirts red. The planked canoes were painted red, and painted boards and poles marked their cemeteries and ceremonial enclosures. Of their color work, nothing remains but the mysterious rock paintings on cliffs and in caverns hidden from the sight of the Spanish in the remote and rugged mountains. Such painted rocks are called pictographs to distinguish them from petroglyphs, which are designs pecked, incised, or abraded in rock.

Location

The pictograph sites are always found near permanent water, either a spring or a running stream. Most of the painted caves occur in the tilted sandstone reefs of the more mountainous country, though several sites in the Santa Monica Mountains and on the islands are in conglomerate and volcanic basalt outcrops. Some are found in high mountain grasslands or *potreros*, others in canyons densely wooded with big-cone spruce, laurel, and alder, but most are in the chaparral belt. A number of finds have been made after forest fires, when for a brief time the impenetrable chaparral is destroyed, revealing the sandstone cave areas.

Kroeber has divided the Chumash country up into dialect zones by drainage areas, and I will roughly follow these divisions in this section. His Barbareño and Island I have combined as Canaliño. Starting down the coast, there is first the Obispeño area, centered around the mission of San Luis Obispo. There are

74

FIGURE 66. Pictograph sites in the Chumash territory. Divisions are based on Kroeber's dialect areas. His Barbareño and Island are here combined as Canaliño.

75

peaks in this area up to 3,000 feet, but the country is generally rolling farmland and cattle range and is drained by a number of short streams. I have recorded two sites from this area.

Next is the Purísimeño section which was under the control of La Purísima Concepción mission. This region has many small coastal streams and the lower parts of the Santa Maria and Santa Ynez rivers. Rock outcrops are few and only four sites are known.

At Point Concepción, the coastline turns to an east-west alignment. From here to near Rincón Point is the Canaliño country, which was dominated by the Santa Barbara mission.

Nearly all the knowledge we have of the ethnographic Chumash comes from this section. It is a region of many short streams dropping into the coastal plain from the steep mountains. Here I have recorded twelve sites. On the islands there are two sites.

Further east is the Ventureño area, controlled by the mission Buenaventura. This country is drained by the Ventura and Santa Clara rivers and numerous short coastal streams. The highest and most mountainous part of the Chumash territory is here, and twelve painted sites are known.

North of the Santa Ynez Mountains is the drainage of the Santa Ynez River. This is the Ynezeño area and was administered by the Santa Inés mission. The valley has many large cattle ranches today, hemmed in by mountains east, north, and south. Eight sites have been recorded here.

Further north is the large Cuyama region. This was a thinly settled area and never under direct mission control. The Sisquoc River, flowing between the San Rafael Range and the Sierra Madre Mountains, drains the southern part, while the broad sandy wash of the Cuyama between the Sierra Madres and the Caliente Range drains the north. Beyond the Calientes lie the arid Carrizo Plains with an interior drainage into Soda Lake. Bounding the plains to the northeast is the Temblor Range, the last of the coastal ranges before the San Joaquin Valley, home of the Yokuts. In the Cuyama I have recorded forty-one painted rock areas.

The last area is the Emigdiano. Remote from any mission influence, it is located in the San Emigdio Range of southwestern Kern County, which drains into the San Joaquin Valley. Here are four known sites.

Subject Matter

There is an almost universal reaction to semi-abstract Indian paintings. The viewer tries to identify some of the design motifs with something within his experience. Some people think that the paintings tell a story that could be read if one only knew the key; others see Egyptian and Masonic symbols! The average person tries to see realistic things like suns, snakes, and insects in the pictures. Such speculations are intriguing but fruitless. The Chumash neither

PLATES

1. Canaliño (SB-12). This small painting on a tilted rock above a spring has design elements integrated in a very sophisticated manner. The creature with the forked tail and some of the dots indicate later overpainting.

1 ft. └─────────────┘

2. Canaliño (SB-21). This is the well-known Painted Cave near San Marcos Pass. It is visited by thousands every year and, thanks to an iron grill closing off the cave entrance, is still in excellent condition.

1 ft. └─────────┘

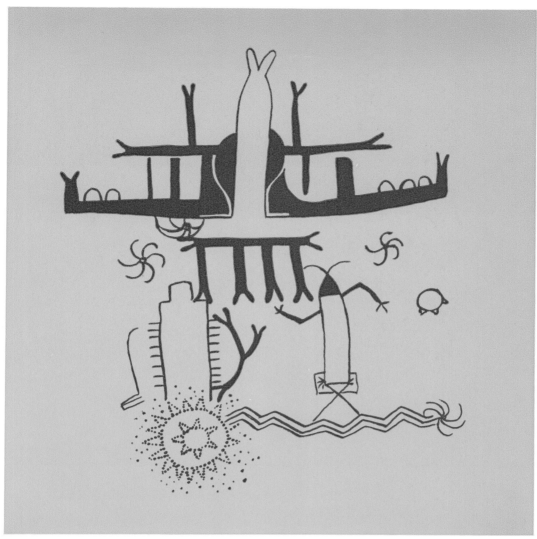

6 in.

5. Cuyama (SL-1B). This pictograph is at the top of the rock in figure 96.

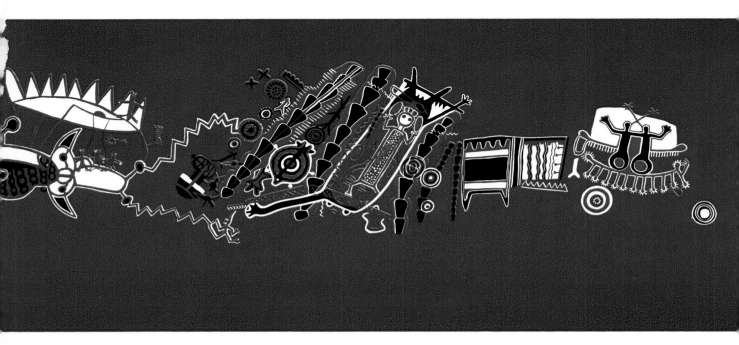

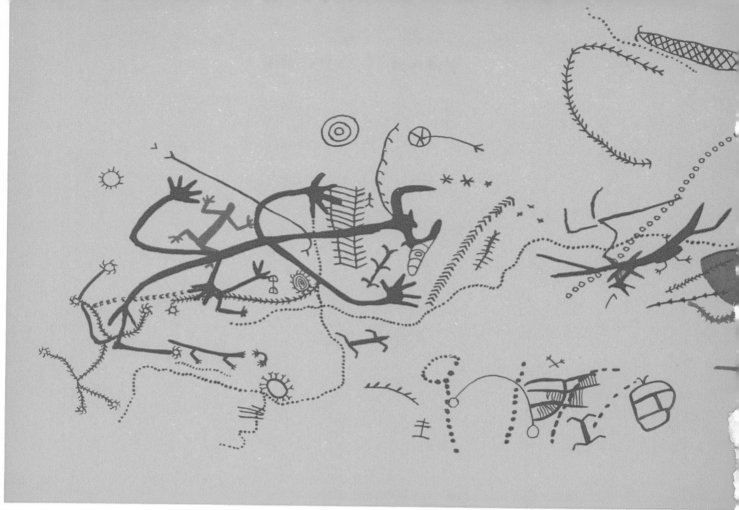

1 ft. └─────────────┘

3. Ynezeño (SB-33). A large painting unlike anything else in the Chumash country. The meandering dots and chevrons suggest a map. The cave opening is tiny and easy to miss, as it is high on a cliff, in heavy brush and timber.

2 ft. └─────────────┘

4. Cuyama (SL-1A). The great painting from the rock shown in figure 96.

6. Cuyama (SL-2). Not in original order. The upper group was in line at the left of the lower group. They were widely spaced along a 60-foot length of cliff. Owing to the lack of protecting overhang, the paintings are in poor condition.

2 ft.

1 ft.

7. Cuyama (SL-4). An elaborate painting found in an unusual location (see figure 100). In order to see this pictograph, one must crawl into a narrow crevice about 36 inches wide and 18 feet deep. Even with a wide-angle lens, it took 37 exposures to record all details. Top left target and two small figures below are not in original order; they have been moved from the far left.

1 ft. └─────────┘

8. Cuyama (SL-5). This site is about 100 feet from that shown in plate 10. Not in original order; the lower figures are to the left of the upper designs.

9. Cuyama (SL-5). A concentric ring design from the same site as plate 8, on cliff face.

1 ft. └─────────┘

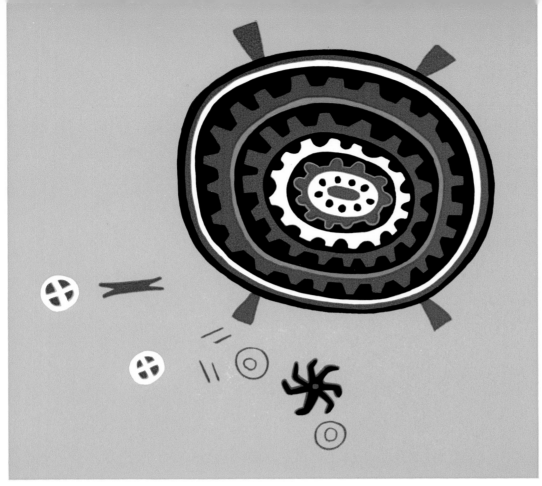

10. Cuyama (SL-5). Painted on cliff face 25 feet from the ground.

1 ft. └─────────────┘

11. Cuyama (SL-5). The flowerlike motifs are unusual in the Chumash area.

1 ft. └─────────────┘

1 ft. └─────────┘

12. Cuyama (KE-3B). Design from the roof of a small cave. Erosion has obliterated the wall detail. The rays on the large fanlike design are incised deeply, then painted.

1 ft. └─────────┘

13. Cuyama (KE-3C). Site on extreme northern edge of Chumash territory, near KE-3B.

14. Cuyama (SB-10). A fine example of dot painting. This is in the same cave as the bear track petroglyph site shown in figure 81.

1 ft.

1 ft.

15. Cuyama (SB-11). These paintings are at the base of the large rock shown in figure 104. Note the headless creatures to the right.

1 ft. └─────────┘

16. Cuyama (SB-17). A small painting from a site showing long occupation, near SB-15.

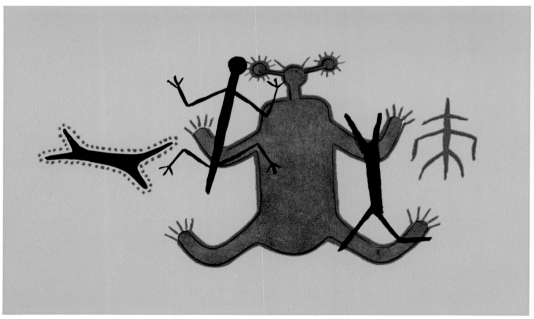

6 in. └─────────┘

17. Cuyama (SB-16). Curious bearlike being, showing superimposition. On a rock lying in a cave.

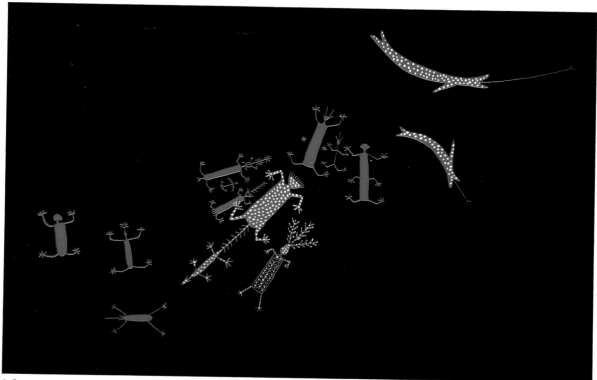

1 ft. └─────────────┘

18. Ventureño (V-1). One of two examples of paintings on a black surface from this large site. Note tongues on the aquatic-looking elements.

1 ft. └─────────────┘

19. Ventureño (V-1). Buglike creatures and a web from the same cave as plate 18.

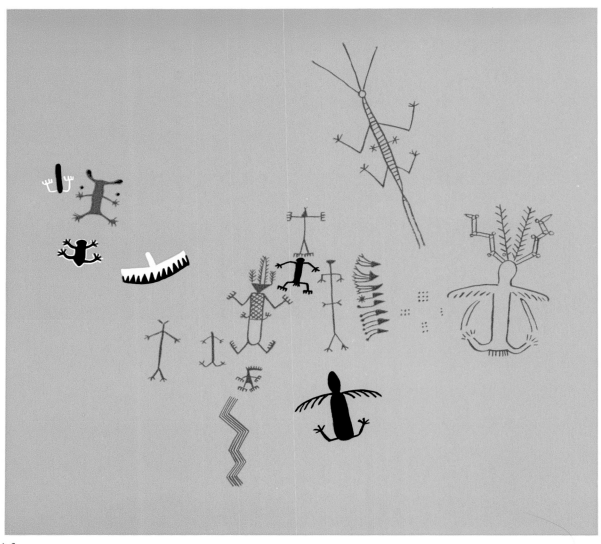

1 ft.

20. Ventureño (V-1). A site characterized by delicacy of paintings and great imagination. Note the two birdlike figures.

21. Ventureño (V-1). More bizarre creatures from this same site, which has eleven caves in a single great rock. In six of the caves the pictures are still legible, but wind erosion has been severe. The birdlike design at bottom left might have been inspired by the condor.

6 in. └────────────┘

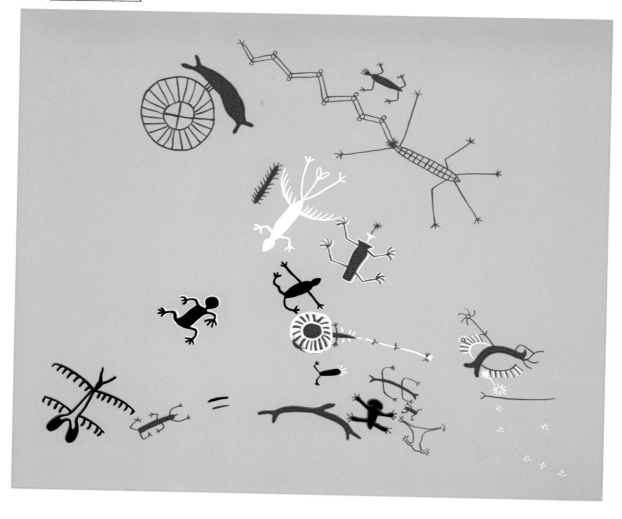

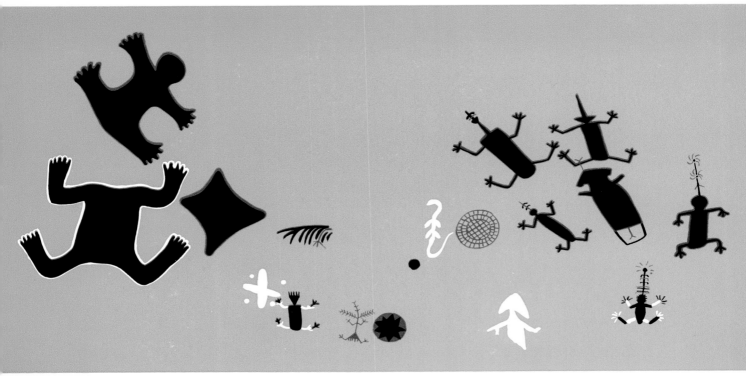

1 ft.

22. Ventureño (V-1). Note beheaded figure at the left. Erosion has erased all but one wing of a bird element. I suspect that the shaman responsible for the pictures at this site had a good sense of humor.

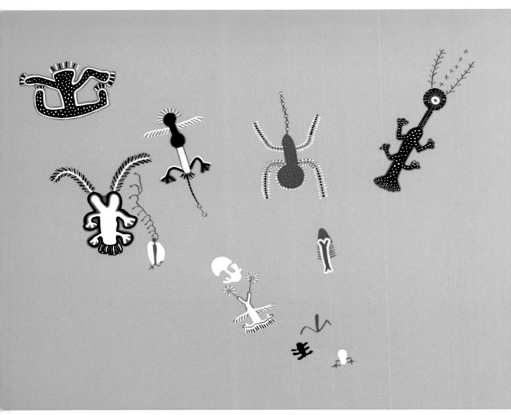

23. Ventureño (V-7). From a site deep in the condor territory, above a permanently flowing stream. The paintings are in the back of a deep cave formed by a rock fall and are in excellent condition.

1 ft.

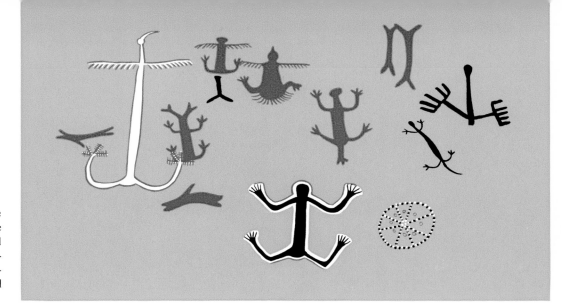

24. Ventureño (V-7). These paintings are about twelve miles by trail from V-1 and show the same gay imagination. The bottom two figures are not in the original order.

1 ft. ⌐_____⌐

25. Ventureño (V-4). There are many unusual elements here—the two comets in upper right, figures with "rake" hands and feet, and people with feathered headdresses at right.

1 ft. ⌐_____⌐

1 ft. ⊢⎯⎯⎯⎯⎯⎯⎯⎯⎯⎯⎯⎯⊣

26. Ventureño (LA-1). This is the only site in Chumash country showing figures
in profile and horsemen.

27. Emigdiano (K-2). The most elaborate and colorful pictograph in Chumash territory. It shows considerable overpainting to the right, where cruder work is overlaid with beautifully executed designs. This painting originally covered most of the cave walls, but the wind has eroded all but these paintings on the roof.

1 ft. └─────────┘

28. Emigdiano (KE-2). Detail of plate 27. Few of the paintings in the Santa Barbara area photograph well because of the ravages of erosion or the impossibility of taking more than a small section in each exposure. This and the following plates are some exceptions.

1 ft. └────────────────┘

6 in. └────────────┘

29. Cuyama (SB-11). Detail of plate 15.

1 ft. |⎣_____⎦|

30. Ventureño (V-4). Detail of plate 25.

1 ft. |⎣_____⎦|

31. Canaliño (SB-21). This shows slight vandalism.

thought as we do, nor did they interpret their ideas as we would. To them the supernatural was as real and as readily visual as the natural. It seems likely that most of the abstract paintings in the Chumash country are visualizations of supernatural beings or forces to be used ceremonially in much the same manner as the Navajo sand figures. Many of their pictures certainly represented things that existed only in the mind of the painter. Others were regional and stylistic formulas to represent objects, creatures, and phenomena known to the shamans of the area. In the western states, there are doubtless some rock pictures that record events, but this does not seem to be true of the southern California abstract pictographs.

There are a number of basic symbols that occur in primitive art throughout the world. Fertility, water, and rain symbols are among the most common, and these appear in the Chumash pictures. The similarity of some of the simplest figures in widely separated continents indicates nothing more than that certain combinations of straight and curved lines suggest the same thing to men everywhere.

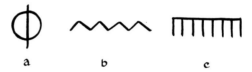

a   b   c

FIGURE 67.   Symbols found throughout the world which occur frequently in Chumash pictographs: a. fertility; b. water; c. rain.

It would be easy if the Chumash drew like Palaeolithic man in Europe or Neolithic man in Africa. Their drawings were superb, almost photographically perfect representations of the animals they knew and hunted. We accept and enjoy them as handsome, perfectly understandable works of art. The prehistoric Chumash have left only paintings that puzzle and intrigue. They are never realistic, are always highly stylized, and often combine elements of known creatures in the most amazing combinations.

Steward (1929) was the first to list Indian design elements according to geographic distribution. His survey covered a very large area—California and adjoining states—and included both pictographs and petroglyphs. He pointed out that the greatest concentration of pictographs in the west was in the Santa Barbara and Tulare areas and that petroglyphs were rare or unknown in these regions. To the east of the Sierra Nevada, the situation was reversed and petroglyphs predominated.

The California Archaeological Survey of the University of California in 1949 listed 40 design elements found in California. I have found 29 of these and an additional 34 in the Chumash country. In figure 69 I have included only elements occurring at more than one site. There are in addition many unique single-example designs.

The few pictographs found along the coastal plain and on the islands, where most of the Chumash lived, are very simple and crude. They are usually made up   77

FIGURE 68. California pictograph and petroglyph design elements. (After Fenenga, 1949)

78

FIGURE 69.   Additional design elements from the Chumash area.

of crisscrosses, rakes, herringbone patterns, sun disks, and are roughly done figures in red. Some are merely chalked on the wall with a piece of hematite. Rarely, there is a well-drawn figure like the swordfish in figure 71.

In the higher country, the designs become increasingly complex and the paintings are often done in polychrome, black, red, and white, with an occasional yellow. The paintings show much imagination and often a sense of humor. In several sites in the Ventureño area are great numbers of fantastic buglike creatures with multiple legs, pinwheel heads, and firework-looking tails. Here too, in

79

what is the last sanctuary of the California condor, there are numbers of birdlike creatures.

In the Cuyama region there are sites where a single rock will have hundreds of designs on it. These for the most part are painted with great care and are marvelously intricate. There are elaborate designs suggesting a sun motif, often with a split center and triangular tags at the four corners. There are many variations on the pinwheel design and humanoid figures with strange bent heads.

In the Emigdiano country is the most complex of all Chumash pictographs. This site has the most amazing polychrome variations on the sun design and weirdly beautiful anthropomorphic beings. The creator, besides being a medicine man, was a first-class artist and innovator and must have derived considerable aesthetic satisfaction from his work.

Of all the design elements, there is only one that seems to be found throughout the entire Chumash territory. It is usually a double-ended design with a split-tail effect at each end (fig. 77). Sometimes the design or creature has a fin in the middle, and in one instance a long forked tongue is attached to one of the ends, giving it the look of an open mouth. This motif, which looks somewhat marine or fishlike, occurs 42 times in 15 sites and is found in six of the seven pictograph areas.

The design elements fall roughly into two groups.

Representational		*Abstract*	
man	insect	square	cross
horseman	salamander	diamond	Maltese cross
bear	turtle	circle	crisscross
deer	horned toad	triangle	wheel
bear track	rattlesnake	dots	target
handprint	lizard	pinwheel	chevron
swordfish	centipede	grid	
bird	flower	zigzag	
bird track	plant	rake	
spider	sun	ladder	
spiderweb	comet	parallel lines	
pelt	star	checkerboard	

In addition there are great numbers of unidentifiable creatures, anthropomorphic and zoomorphic figures, and curious abstract designs that only a picture can describe. The paintings of animate forms are almost invariably done in a flat or "spread eagle" manner. I have recorded only two instances of attempts at realism—the swordfish on page 81 from the Purisimeño area and the four horsemen (pl. 26) from the Ventureño region.

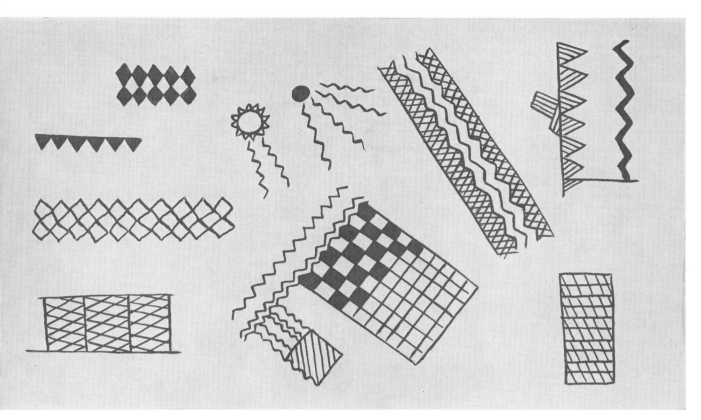

FIGURE 70. Design elements from two sites in the Obispeño area. Red only.

FIGURE 71. Design elements from three sites in the Purísimeño area. Red and black.

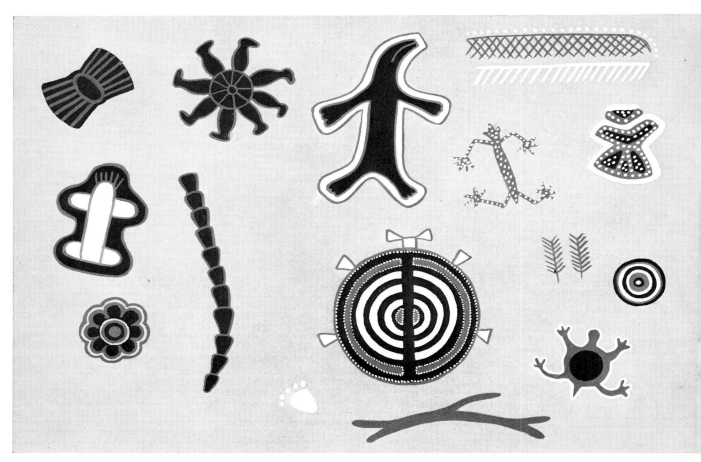

FIGURE 72. Design elements from eight sites in the Cuyama area. Black, red, white, and yellow.

FIGURE 73. Design elements from four sites in the Emigdiano area. Red, black, white, yellow, orange, blue, and green.

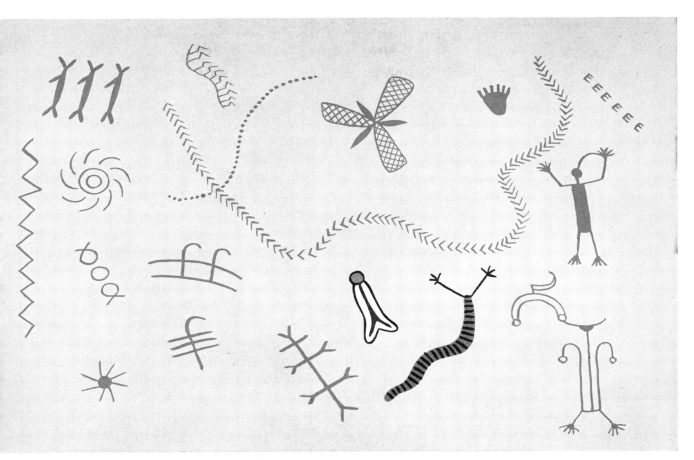

FIGURE 74. Design elements from five sites in the Yneześo area. Black, red, and white.

FIGURE 75. Design elements from five sites in the Ventureño area. Black, red, and white.

FIGURE 76.   Design elements from seven sites in the Canaliño area. Red, black, and white.

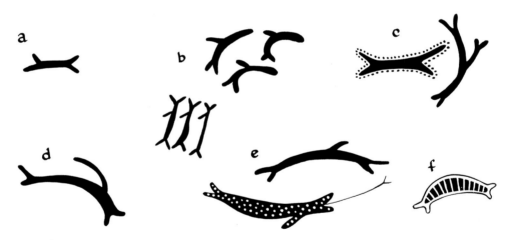

FIGURE 77.   The aquatic design from nine sites in the Chumash country. a. Purísimeño; b. Yne-zeño; c. Cuyama; d. Canaliño; e. Ventureño; f. Emigdiano.

Pigments, Techniques, and Styles

All the colors used by the Indian painters were earth colors, the most permanent of pigments. Though the pictographs will flake off and weather away, in well-protected sites the colors are as brilliant as when first applied.

84

The red paint found at nearly all pictograph sites is the iron oxide, hematite, and occurs in shades from dull red to bright vermilion. Earthy hematite is found in only a few locations in California and is usually of a dull brownish red color. The northeastern Paiute and the Cocopa Indians near the Mexican border intensified the natural color of the ore by exposing it to fire, the oxidizing effect of the flames on the hematite turning it a bright brick red. The yellow paint is limonite, another iron oxide, and is found in colors ranging from yellow ochre to dull orange. The best white was made from diatomaceous earth, of which there is a large deposit near Lompoc. A lump of black paint found near Santa Barbara was analyzed and found to be the hydrous oxide of manganese. In some cases ordinary charcoal may have been used but the finest black was made of burned graphite by the Yokuts and was undoubtedly traded with the neighboring Chumash. At three sites I have found blue and green in the paintings. Certain shades of these colors were probably derived from local deposits of serpentine.

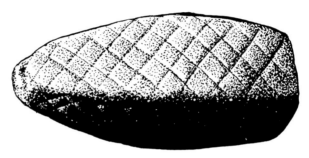

FIGURE 78. Molded and incised paint cake of hematite from the Cuyama area. Length, 4½ inches. (Santa Barbara Museum of Natural History)

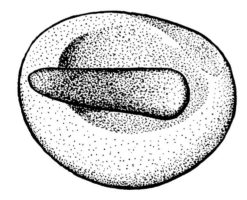

FIGURE 79.
Sandstone paint mortar and pestle. The original is heavily stained with hematite. Diameter, 4½ inches. (Southwest Museum)

The Yokuts method of preparing the black paint was to gather a quantity of crude graphite from an area of decomposed granite. This was put into a hole in a bed of hot coals and covered with more coals. By the time the fire burned down, the graphite had become a fine, sooty black powder. The other pigment materials were reduced to powder in paint mortars. The paints were then wetted and pressed into balls and cakes to be stored for future use. The Yokuts molded their paint into balls the size of tennis balls which were a standard paint measure for trading. The Chumash kept their colors in square, oblong, round, and conical pieces.

85

For paint cups along the coast, vertebrae of large fish and shells were used, but in the mountains the painter often pecked out small depressions in the rock where he was working. The remnants of paint can still be seen in some of these little rock cups.

For ceremonial paint for their bodies, the Indians obviously used water to mix with the pigments, but for the rock painting, oil was added to the color to make a permanent waterproof paint. It is not known exactly what type of binder the Chumash added to their pigment, but it is reasonably certain that it was the same or similar to that of the Yokuts. These Indians made their binder of the juice of the milkweed (*Asclepias fascicularis*) mixed with oil extracted from the crushed seeds of the chilicothe (*Echinocystis macrocarpa*). It is also likely that animal oil and the whites of bird's egg were sometimes used.

To apply the paint, the Chumash used brushes, probably made of frayed yucca fiber or the outer husks of the soap plant *Chlorogalum*. The latter was used by the southern Yokuts painters. Other methods of applying color were by a sharpened stick, the finger, and, in some coastal areas, simply drawing on the rock surface with a lump of hematite.

FIGURE 80.
Soap plant fiber brush found in a Chumash cave. Such brushes were hair or utility brushes, and smaller forms were used for painting. Length, 4½ inches. (Santa Barbara Museum of Natural History)

The techniques used by the creators of the paintings differed from area to area. In the Obispeño region, the paintings are simple red linear designs. The Purisimeño pictographs are usually drawn directly on the sandstone with lump pigment, but there is some simple brushwork in red and black. In the Canaliño country, the drawing is sometimes scratched through the smoke blackening to the raw rock surface. The usual technique was a simple brushwork in red, occasionally black and white and rarely polychrome, while in numbers of caves, outlines are indicated with dots. The Ynezeño area designs are red linear. The coastal Ventureño paintings are mainly red and crudely done, some suggesting finger painting. Further inland, the work is more facile with a palette of red, black, white, and yellow. Many paintings are delicately executed with a fine brush or stick. In the Cuyama and Emigdiano areas, the paintings reach a maximum complexity with intricate multi-bordered and dot-elaborated figures. The extraordinary polychrome pictograph in red, black, white, yellow, green, and blue illustrated in plates 27–28 is from the latter region. This painting, done over an earlier, far cruder polychrome, is certainly the work of a single artist, far surpassing in invention and execution anything else in the Chumash country.

There is a great variation in the skill and imagination shown in the paintings. Though some basic elements are similar over large areas, the great richness of detail at one site and the basic simplicity of design elements in another cave not too far away seem to indicate that some medicine men could draw and others could not, that some had vivid imaginations and others did not.

The various styles break down into three main types and two subtypes. At each painted site one of these types will predominate but is usually found in association with one or more other styles. At a few sites, *all* these styles occur side by side, in combination or superimposition. Only Type II and IIA ever appear alone.

Painting Styles

Type I Outline style	Polychrome painting with elements outlined with a contrasting color. There are often multiple outlines, especially of "cog wheel" designs.
Type II Linear red style	The most common style in the Santa Barbara region.
Type IIA Linear black or white	Usually occurs with Type II—not common.
Type III Dotted style	Outlines indicated with dots.
Type IIIA Dotted polychrome style	Dot style applied to Type I as elaboration.

At most (53) of the Santa Barbara area sites, Type II is the dominant style, and at 41 of these sites only Type II occurs. Type I is dominant at 17 sites; Type IIA, at 13 sites; Type III, at 2 sites; and Type IIIA, at 3 sites. In the Cuyama and Emigdiano regions, contact zones with tribes to the northeast and east, there are 3 major sites where all of the painting styles are found.

Petroglyphs (peckings on rock) are rare in the Chumash country. At one site in the Ynezeño area, there is a large serpentine rock covered with pecked holes about an inch in diameter, incised grooves, and one small human figure. This is very similar to the typical cup and groove rocks found in many parts of the world. Heizer (1953) has described rocks of this type in northern California, where they are known as rain rocks. They also occur in the Sierra foothills. In the Cuyama region, there are several sites with pecked holes in straight and meandering lines and one remarkable cave where forty-nine bear tracks are either carved into the rock or scratched through the smoke-blackened surface to the bare rock beneath. On San Nicolás Island (inhabited by a Shoshonean-speaking people with a Canaliño culture), there are a few black pictographs and some fine incised petroglyphs of killer whales. (See Appendix A.)

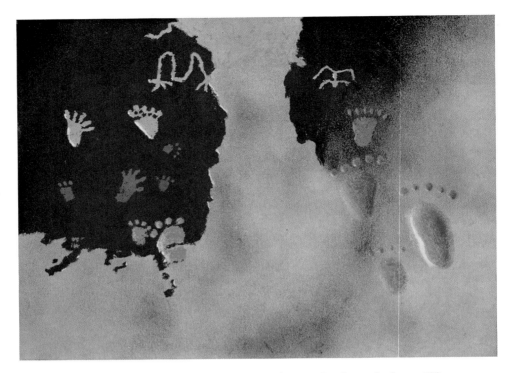

FIGURE 81. Bear track petroglyph in the Cuyama region, at site shown in figure 103.

FIGURE 82. "Rain rock" petroglyph from Santa Ynez Mountains.

What Do They Mean?

Although many of the pictographs are aesthetically pleasing, they cannot conceivably have been done as "art for art's sake." Most cave art, from the Palaeolithic paintings of 15,000 years ago to the aboriginal paintings still being done in some parts of Australia, undoubtedly has a magical or religious significance.

In a search for meaning in the Chumash pictographs, several puzzling questions arise. Why are these paintings almost always confined to the mountains? It is true that most of the sandstone caves are in the higher country, but not all are by any means. Were they in the nature of shrines or sacred places to which the coastal and valley people made pilgrimage? Were they done almost entirely by small bands of mountain Chumash? To help reach some possible answer, it is necessary to have a closer look at the sites.

These caves or rock shelters were in no sense living quarters, although they doubtless gave occasional shelter from rain and cold. I have seen one cave almost 50 feet deep, but the average depth is six to ten feet. Around most sites are bedrock mortars. At one site, a few yards from a painting, there is a large flat outcrop with 21 of these holes varying in size from a few inches in diameter to over a foot wide and ten inches deep. The few prehistoric baskets and wooden objects that have been preserved were found in these caves.

FIGURE 83.
Bedrock mortar holes near a Canaliño site.

89

THE PAINTINGS

Near many sites there is no flat land suitable for erecting houses, and at others only a small area of such land is available. Such sites could have been occupied by a small family group, no more. At several larger sites, much midden is present but no sign of houses. Later excavation may prove whether the high mountain sites had permanent settlements nearby or only summer encampments.

At a spectacular site in the Cuyama area, there is an immense rock about 60 feet high and formed like a horseshoe, creating a natural amphitheater. Inside the rock are a great many fine paintings, badly vandalized. Ancient trails wind up the surface of the rock, and at the top there are more paintings, including the mysterious fishlike design. The amphitheater could easily hold hundreds of people, and it is not difficult to imagine fires burning in the center, lighting some ceremonial dance while great numbers of Indians gathered from the surrounding country to watch from the gallery above. Near this picture rock is a village site and a cemetery.

In Australia, rock paintings are still being done for use in religious ceremonies, and the medicine men of the Navajo are making sand paintings today following an ancient tradition. It seems certain that most of the paintings in the Chumash area were the creation of the shamans and were for the ceremonial use of particular regional groups. The smaller pictograph sites may have served the supernatural needs of a single family unit, while the large sites were used by sizeable villages. Plate 29 shows a person, possibly a hostile shaman, in headdress, and four creatures with no heads. This site could have been used ceremonially to destroy or protect from these beings. The headlessness suggests that they were killed.

In the Luiseño and Cupeño areas of southern California, we know the meaning and purpose of the pictographs. The Luiseño girls were put through an elaborate puberty ceremony. They spent three days in a pit with heated rocks. On the morning of the fourth day, they were taken from the pit and their faces were painted black for a month. The second month, vertical white lines were painted on their faces, and the third month, wavy, red horizontal lines. After ceremonies involving ground painting, the girls raced to a certain rock, where red pigment was given them by relatives and they painted diamond-shaped designs representing the rattlesnake on the rock. The Cupeño ceremony was almost exactly the same. There are many paintings in that area where a wavy line and the diamond are almost the only designs. In the Salinan country bordering the Chumash to the northeast and extending somewhat into what may be Chumash territory, are similar designs, all linear zigzags, parallel lines, and grids. It is possible that these served a similar purpose to those in the Luiseño country.

Kroeber, in 1925 (p. 938), when knowledge of California pictographs was slight, wrote:

> The cave paintings of the south, therefore, represent a particular art, a local style or cult. This can be connected, in all probability, with the technological art of the Chumash and island Shoshoneans, as manifest in the occasional carvings of whales, quadrupeds, and the like in steatite. Since these paintings further fall well within the region of the toloache religion, in fact their distribution coincides

rather closely with the area in which this religion was strongest, and since its cult was in certain tracts worked out in visible symbols such as the sand painting, an association with this religion is also to be considered, although nothing positive is known in the matter. Many of the pictures may have been made by shamans; and it is quite possible that medicine men were not connected with the making of any.

The latter part of this statement is wondrously hedged but shows the bafflement of the best men in the field on this difficult subject. In 1929, Steward groped in another direction. Were they doodles or was there a meaning? In his excellent *Petroglyphs of California* (pp. 224–225) he says:

> Innumerable attempts have been made to ascertain the meanings of petroglyphs and pictographs from Indians living at present in the region where they occur. These have invariably met with failure. The Indians disclaim all knowledge of their meaning and origin. In many instances, the Indians are aware of the inscriptions and often regard them with fear.
>
> The meaning and purpose of petroglyphs and pictographs can only be ascertained through careful study of art and symbolism of present Indian groups and a comparison of these with petrographic elements.
>
> It has frequently been stated that the petroglyphs and pictographs are meaningless figures made in idle moments by some primitive artist. The facts of distribution, however, show that this cannot be true. Since design elements and style are grouped in limited areas, the primitive artist must have made the inscriptions with something in mind. He must have followed a pattern of petrography which was in vogue in his area. He executed, not random drawings, but figures similar to those made in other parts of the same area. The elements of design, then, must have had some definite significance which was the same over wide areas.

In 1949, F. F. Latta published his *Handbook of the Yokuts Indians*. It was the result of over thirty years of close study of these people. The Yokuts of the San Joaquin Valley were the only other Indian group in California making extensive pictographs similar to their neighbors, the Chumash. The Yokuts paintings were done in the Sierra Nevada foothills on granite; the Chumash, on sandstone. Both painted in red, black, white, and yellow, in abstract and, rarely, naturalistic forms. Latta interviewed over two hundred Indians (some of whom may have had Chumash blood, as many missionized and mountain Chumash fled to the San Joaquin during and after the mission period and never returned). These people told Latta many things pertinent to the Chumash, including the first positive word from Indian sources on the pictographs. The fragmentary gleanings are worth quoting.

> *Sok-só-uh* is the name of a bad, supernatural spirit, and was applied to the large figure on the ceiling of the Painted Rock at Tule River Indian Reservation. This painting resembles the stretched skin of a mountain lion holding the sun in its mouth. (*Ibid.*, p. 24)
>
> These Wukchumne Indians said the paintings were generally placed at an important village site, one which was permanently inhabited or at some place where Indian ceremonies were performed. They stated that tribal equipment,

91

such as symmetrical mortars and pestles for grinding Indian tobacco, or costumes for tribal ceremonies were often concealed near these paintings. The idea furnished was that the paintings added prestige to the spot and served to awe the lesser characters of the tribe and instill in them a respect for the equipment concealed there. The Wukchumne stated that such places were *Trip'-ne* (supernatural). Red paintings such as are common at Hospital Rock were called *Haw-you.* Paintings using mixed colors were called *Hoo'-cha-ing-utch.* The Indians readily recognize the characters which represent animals, but they offer no other explanation for the geometrical designs and line drawings . . . In exception to this they do identify drawings of the sun, moon and *Chapet* (Cha'-peet— the Indian doctor's magic tray), and a few mythological characters. (*Ibid.,* pp. 179–180)

FIGURE 84. Sok-so'-uh, an evil supernatural spirit from the ceiling of Painted Rock at the Tule River Indian Reservation. This is an example of vandalism through chalk outlining of painting by enthusiastic black-and-white photographers.

To verify one point brought out here, a superb ceremonial dance skirt made of crow and eagle feathers has been found in a cave in the Cuyama area near a pictograph site.

In April, 1963, I had the opportunity of spending a day with Professor Herbert Kühn at the site shown in plates 4 and 5. Kühn, a friend and associate of the Abbé Breuil, teaches prehistory at the University of Mainz and is the foremost authority on the rock art of Europe. In his opinion, the Chumash paintings depict, not things but concepts—the concepts of good and evil that have pre-occupied man since the beginning. These forces were represented differently in different places by the medicine men but were readily understandable to the people of their regions. In ceremonies involving dancing, singing, and sometimes the use of tobacco and narcotics, appeals were made to the forces of good to supply the needed things, such as health, fertility, and rain; the powers of evil, causing sickness, sterility, drought, and other undesirable things, were exorcised.

How Old Are They?

This is a difficult question and may never have a very satisfactory answer. However, it is possible to reach some general conclusions from the evidence. It is certain that they were painted over a period of time, as there are a number of examples of superimposition (see pl. 27 and 30). The predominant red linear style (Type II) occurs at nine sites under later Type I and IIA. At one site, a crude polychrome pictograph is overpainted by a later, more skillfully executed polychrome. How much older the underpaintings may be than the overpaintings is impossible to determine, but the numerous examples of Type II and IIA are generally fainter and more eroded than the other painting styles.

The greatest concentration of pure Type II is along the coast (including two sites on the islands), while Type I dominates in the northern semi-desert Chumash borderland, suggesting that the polychrome style was introduced at a later time from adjoining tribes, particularly the Yokuts. In the Yokuts territory, there are many examples of the polychrome outlined style.

The paints were mixed with an animal or vegetable oil binder, and this may eventually help to give us some dates. Dr. Willard Libby's radiocarbon method of dating organic material can be used if enough paint fragments can be recovered from eroding sites. I recently collected a sample of paint from a badly eroded site and Dr. Libby ran a radiocarbon test on the material. The amount of organic matter remaining after the sample had been refined was so slight (only about 5% of the usual amount of material needed) that the test was inconclusive. The indications were that the binder in the paint was anywhere from 100 to 2000 years old.

The difficulties of trying to date with this method are twofold: It may never be possible to recover enough paint material for an ideal test, from a site, short of destroying the site, and (2) the Chumash undoubtedly refreshed and touched up important paintings. This practice has been followed in recent times by Australian aborigines, and a radiocarbon date might merely indicate the time of the last overpainting.

I have recorded one pictograph at the extreme eastern edge of the Chumash territory which shows the usual lizardlike, manlike, and birdlike creatures. At the top of the cave are four horsemen in profile. This would definitely seem to place the painting in mission times. On the other hand, they may have been   93

THE PAINTINGS

done in the mid-1500's. When Cabrillo landed in 1542, the Chumash gave him excellent descriptions of the armored Spanish horsemen of Coronado's expedition seen in Arizona the previous year. News of these astonishing people had traveled to the coastal tribes through trade channels or by roving bands of the Colorado River Mojaves.

The rate of erosion is extremely variable, depending on exposure to wind and moisture. A pictograph site recorded by Mallery and illustrated with many drawings in the Bureau of Ethnology report of 1893 is now almost entirely destroyed through erosion. A pictograph near Santa Barbara, also pictured by Mallery, remains unchanged today.

Several sites have pictographs covered with lichens. The slow growth of these plants is shown in several locations where old Indian trails and footholds cross lichen-covered ledges. Though almost two centuries have elapsed since some of these were last used, no lichen has grown back.

In 1963, two important collections of artifacts from the immediate vicinity of painted sites were acquired by the Santa Barbara Museum of Natural History. These collections from the Cuyama area—one from a burial site and the other from adjacent dry caves—are clearly late Canaliño with a rather complete selec-

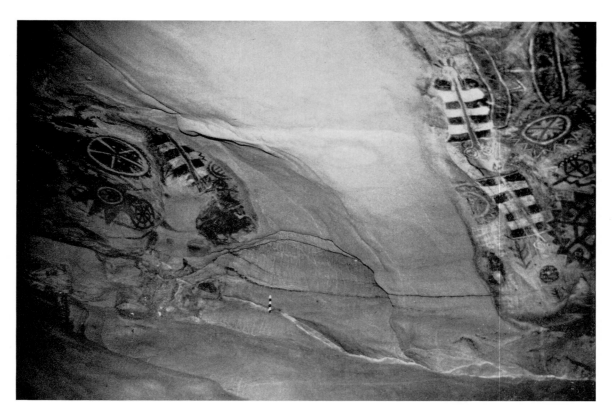

FIGURE 85. A good example of damage through wind erosion. The right section is the left end of plate 2. The narrow cave opening has limited the effect of the prevailing northwest wind to a six-foot-wide section in the back of the cave, neatly erasing a large part of the painting.

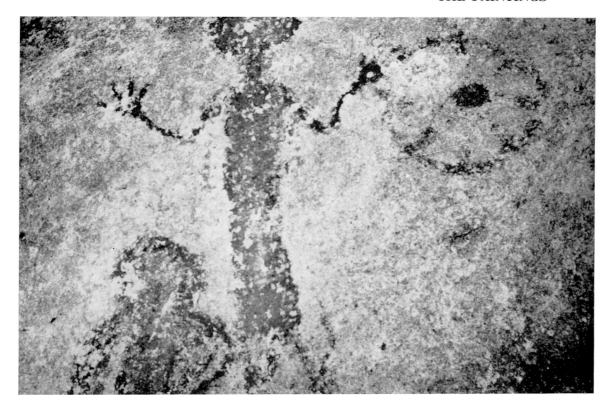

FIGURE 86. A detail of the painting in plate 7. This shows rock decay and damage to the painting by exfoliation.

FIGURE 87. This old Indian trail crosses lichen-covered sandstone. The cliff in the background is the painted surface in plate 6.

95

tion of typical coastal Canaliño material. A basket fragment from one of the caves has been radiocarbon-dated as 120 years old. Both caves and burials included Spanish contact items (mission period, 1772–1833). Orr (1960) has described a late Canaliño site from Santa Rosa Island (Santa Barbara area) which is 1,860 years old. The artifact material near these caves is almost entirely of late Canaliño culture, so that a strong case can be made that these are the people who painted the pictures.

Excavations in the Cuyama area within a few hundred feet of the painting in plate 7 have uncovered burials, flexed and with head to the west. These burials, containing quantities of clamshell beads and abalone pendants, look like late Canaliño again. The excavation by Deetz and Dethlefsen (see Deetz, 1964) at Alamo Pintado, an inland Canaliño site, exposed a rock with a group of centipede-like creatures painted on it in red. The creatures (perhaps representing bad spirits) had been "killed" with a generous smear of melted asphalt. The site is late, with much Spanish contact material.

The evidence seems to indicate that the paintings were done within the last 1,000 years, with a strong probability that they were still being made down to the start of the mission period.

Erosion and Vandalism

There is no known site that has not suffered to some extent from erosion. This is natural and inevitable. Most of the paintings are on sandstone, which can vary in texture from coarse granular to a dense and compact surface that is almost as erosion-resistant as basalt. In sheltered spots such as narrow wooded canyons, the cave pictures are in remarkably good condition. Where the rock outcrop faces a prevailing wind or is in open chaparral and grassland, erosion is severe. A few pictographs are on shale, volcanic rock, or conglomerate. These show the least effect of erosion.

There are different types of erosion at work in this slow destruction. The worst is wind action—the same wind that may have scoured out the cave itself. In the Canaliño area there is a pictograph about 25 feet long. A six-foot section in the center is completely gone, while the two end sections are almost as fresh as the day they were painted. The eroded part exactly lines up with the narrow cave entrance and has been subject to centuries of northwest winds. The second type of erosion is through water, which seeps into some caves and works to weaken and break down the rock surface, often causing flaking or exfoliation of thin layers of rock.

The white coloring is always the first to disappear, followed by the black and yellow. The red paint is the most durable and erosion-resistant of the Indian pigments. Where all paint has flaked away or has been wind-scoured from the surface, a red stain penetrating the surface will remain, giving a faint but accurate image of the former painted areas.

96   Damage through vandalism is a far greater threat to the existence of these

FIGURE 88. Right section of painting shown in plate 4. This picture was taken in the 1870's.

FIGURE 89. The same view, taken in 1961. The damage here is all by gunfire, though in other parts of the same pictograph the vandalism is chiefly in the form of carved, scribbled, and painted names.

pictographs than erosion. Wherever the sites are near roads or trails, the vandal goes to work. There is a moronic segment of any population who, when faced with evidences of ancient peoples, gain some atavistic pleasure by scrawling their names and dates across the wall or painted surface. The enduring stone must testify not only to the skill of the unknown Indian artist but to the fact that Joe Reilly of Oil City, California, was there on June 7, 1956. This destructive urge seems incurable—the Roman soldiers were scratching their names on Egyptian temples in Caesar's time. The modern vandal has the advantage of firearms to help complete the ruin.

Another form of vandalism is the chalking of designs to bring out details for black-and-white photography. This is a deplorable habit, never giving more than the crudest idea of the original pictograph and ruining the painting for serious study. It is next to impossible to remove the chalk without damage to the painting. This practice is sometimes defensible on exposed rock *carvings*, which under certain light conditions are difficult to photograph. The chalk can be removed without damage to the carving. Unfortunately, few chalkers bother to remove the chalk.

The painting reproduced on plate 4 is my restoration of a superb pictograph in the Cuyama area. It is over 40 feet long and has been almost completely destroyed in the last few decades by rifle fire and hundreds of carved, painted, and scribbled names. My painting is based on a set of black-and-white photographs taken in the 1870's and early 1900's together with color slides of the wall in its present condition.

Methods of Recording

When a site has been located, I make notes on elevation, kind of rock, size of painted area, design elements, erosion, vandalism, and so forth. All this information is later transferred to a site description sheet—(see fig. 90) and a precise location of it made on a topographic map so that the site may be readily relocated. Due to the long distances traveled to most sites, often on foot through heavy chaparral, my equipment is as simple and light as possible. The camera I use is a Leica model 111f with a wide-angle lens, either the *28 mm Summaron* or the *35 mm Summaron*. The location of most paintings makes the wide-angle lens a necessity. At one site, I had to crawl into a cleft in the rock not over 2½ feet wide. Inside the cleft was the painting reproduced on plate 7. It was 15 feet long and so close to the camera at all points that it took 37 exposures to cover it.

The caves are usually quite shallow, allowing a fair amount of light on the painted surface, but to eliminate shadows and obtain the greatest clarity of detail, I use supplementary light. The compact Braun Hobby electronic flash will take about 40 pictures for each of the rechargeable batteries. I sometimes take pictures by daylight with a 50 Summarit f/1.5 lens. I began with regular daylight Kodachrome but now use the faster Kodachrome II.

FIGURE 90. Pictograph record sheet. These records are kept on all sites.

SANTA BARBARA MUSEUM OF NATURAL HISTORY
PICTOGRAPH SURVEY RECORD

1. SITE Painted Cave   2. NUMBER CGSB-21   3. COUNTY Santa Barbara
4. MAP USGS San Raphael Mt. 1943, T5N–28W–523
5. ELEVATION 2,600 feet
6. LOCATION Below Painted Cave resort on west fork of Mario Ignacio Creek.

7. DIMENSIONS OF PAINTED AREA   5 x 12 feet
8. KIND OF ROCK Sandstone
9. POSITION OF ROCK Faces north
10. COLORS Red, white, and black
11. DESIGN ELEMENTS   13 15 17 20 21 36 38 43 77 78

12. SUPERIMPOSITION Yes
13. EROSION Slight.
14. VANDALISM Slight (cave has been protected for many years by an iron grille).
15. ASSOCIATED FEATURES Oaks Laurels creek 75 feet below.

16. REMARKS This is the first site in the region to come to the notice of archaeologists.
      Sketched in 1875 by Stephen Bowers. Southwest Museum MS.
17. PREVIOUS DESIGNATIONS FOR SITE Steward site 83 PC, (U. C.) SB 506.
18. PUBLISHED REFERENCES Mallery (1886, 1893), Steward (1929).
19. RECORDED BY Campbell Grant
20. DATE June, 1960   21. PHOTOS Color slides

FIGURE 91. The author photographing the painting shown in plate 10. I much prefer the use of
    artificial light, as sunlight picks up all the irregularities of the rock surface, but here I had
    no choice.

FIGURE 92. An undecipherable painted surface before water treatment. The cast shadow intensifies the problem. Note the beer can, trademark of the vandal. This is part of the great site shown in plate 4.

In shooting a large pictograph, I overlap each exposure slightly so the various parts of the painting can be related to one another later. An assistant holds a six-inch marker in each picture field as a constant scale guide. Sometimes the painting is almost entirely hidden under a calcareous deposit. A fine spray of water from a hand spray tank or water applied with a sponge from a canteen will bring the colors back long enough to photograph. Where erosion has nearly destroyed a pictograph, a pencil drawing is made on the spot to record details too dim for the camera to pick up.

In my studio, the colored slides are projected onto large sheets of white paper and carefully traced. They are then transferred onto drawing paper, buff, gray, or black, approximating the color of the sandstone or the smoke-blackened surfaces so often preferred by the Chumash artist. The facsimile painting is done in gouache or tempera.

I have no interest in faithfully reproducing surface patina or the ravages of erosion or vandalism; the photograph can do this far more quickly and better. My paintings show as accurately as possible the appearance of the pictographs at the time they were painted. This is the method of Breuil in his superb paintings of European Palaeolithic cave art. I used this method in making the first paintings of the Bonompak murals in southern Mexico for Giles Healy, the discoverer, in 1947, as did Antonio Tejeda in his later complete record of that great site.

100

FIGURE 93. The same location photographed after water application.

SOME CHARACTERISTIC SITES

Abbreviations used in site designations:

KE Kern County	SB Santa Barbara County	V Ventura County
LA Los Angeles County	SL San Luis Obispo County	

FIGURE 94. (KE-2) The cave shown at the top of the big rock in the center of the picture contains the most elaborate of all known pictographs in the United States. It is shown in plates 27 and 28 and the frontispiece. Nearby are several other rock paintings, of a much simpler and cruder nature. This is an area of oak and grassland.

101

FIGURE 95. (SL-5) This huge rock mass (note car, lower left) was the background for many widely separated pictographs. Plates 8–11 show some of them. Along the cliff face are over thirty bedrock mortars. The plant life is of a semi-desert type—juniper, desert tea, chamise, and so on.

FIGURE 96. (SL-1) This is the badly vandalized site shown in figures 88, 89, 92, and 93, and plates 4 and 5. Its location in open country near traveled roads has doomed it to destruction. The rock is nearly 100 feet high, and formed in a U shape. The dark shadow is the west and unpainted side of a natural amphitheater. Visible on the rock surface are the deeply worn Indian paths to the summit.

102

FIGURE 97. (V-1) This rock rises from a mountain meadow surrounded by pines, and a year-round creek winds by the base. Lateral clefts cut through the rock mass in a number of places and give access to the painted areas, six in all. The paintings from this site are shown in plates 18–22. There were many bedrock mortars and basket mortar bases at this spot.

FIGURE 98. (V-4) The painting shown in plate 25 lies directly behind the man on the right. This is in an area of several square miles of highly eroded sandstone. The tilted sandstone reefs shown in the photograph are characteristic of many sites. The region is one of sage and yucca with few springs and no summer-running streams.

103

FIGURE 99.
(LA-1) The paintings here (see pl. 26) are in the dark area behind the standing figure. The rock is a conglomerate with few good painting surfaces. Oak, pine, and chaparral are the common plants nearby.

FIGURE 100.   (SL-4) The young man in the rock cleft is standing beside the large painting shown in plate 7. The painting extends back some 15 feet into the narrowing cleft, making photography extremely difficult. The rattlesnakes shown in the painting are still very active near this site.

FIGURE 101.   (SB-12) This site lies at the headwaters of a coastal stream in
dense thickets of laurel, scrub oak, and poison oak. The arrowhead-
shaped calcium deposit on the tilted rock points downward to a good
spring where the boy is standing. A few feet away was a bedrock mortar
with the pestle still in place.

FIGURE 102. (SB-33) This site was reached after a most exhausting trip. Carrying packs and cutting our way down a brush-choked arroyo with machetes, we made a mile in two hours. The cave opening shown to the right of my son was only 16 inches wide, opening up to a height of four feet inside. A creek is directly below the rock face, kept running in the driest months by a large spring. The painting from this site is shown in plate 3.

FIGURE 103. (SB-10) This location is several air miles from SB-11 in the same sandstone formation. This rock contains five painted caves, one of them the bearpaw petroglyph site pictured in figure 81. There are many hand and toeholds cut into the steeper parts of the rock, and over twenty bedrock mortars. Note man for scale.

106

FIGURE 104. (SB-11) A very remote site in the heavy chaparral zone. The molar-shaped rock is over 75 feet high with a sizeable pine growing in windblown sand at the top. Carved toeholds lead up the center depression to a natural cistern at the top left. In a wet year this will store several thousands of gallons of water. At the base of the rock are a number of wind-eroded caves and bedrock mortar holes. Plate 15 shows the painted designs from this site.

Comparisons with Other Areas

Cave paintings (pictographs) and carvings or peckings (petroglyphs) are found throughout the world. The smooth rock surfaces of caves first challenged man's imagination and talents over 15,000 years ago. The Palaeolithic cave art in France and Spain represents the first attempts to create something beyond the bare needs of existence.

Since the first awakening of interest in pictographs, after the discovery of the famous cave of Altamira in Spain, literally thousands of sites have been recorded. The major pictograph and petroglyph areas of the world are Europe (France, Spain and Italy), Africa, Australia, and North America.

North America

In the United States, the painted sites are heavily concentrated in the western states, with very few examples east of the Mississippi. In 1946, there were eight eastern states without recorded pictographs or petroglyphs. Generally the pecked or carved designs predominate, but there are two notable exceptions.

107

THE PAINTINGS

The first is the great concentration of Indian rock painting in southwest Texas. Here the pictographs outnumber the petroglyphs five to one. The other is California south of San Francisco, where there are almost no petroglyphs west of the Sierra Nevada. In the Great Basin area, east of the Sierra barrier, the situation is reversed and the pictograph becomes the rare form. The type of rock determines to a great extent the petroglyph zones. Rock peckings are the common form in areas of abundant basaltic rock. When the dark surface is broken by the pecking stone, the design shows up plainly as a much lighter color. Neither granite or sandstone are ordinarily suited to the delineation of complex pecked designs. The Santa Barbara and Tulare areas, together with southwest Texas, are by far the richest pictograph regions known in North America.

On the map (fig. 105) I have rather arbitrarily divided the country into six pictograph zones. The divisions are basically geographic, but culture areas have also been considered in drawing the boundaries. The most difficult line to draw

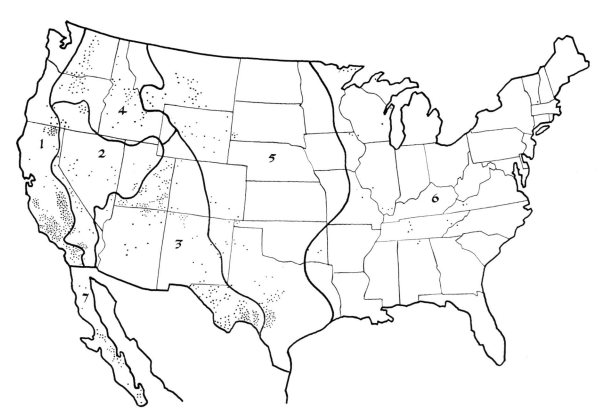

FIGURE 105. The major pictograph areas of the United States (including Baja California). 1. Pacific Coast. 2. Great Basin. 3. Southwest. 4. Columbia Plateau. 5. Great Plains. 6. Eastern Woodland. 7. Baja California. The dots indicating sites can only give a rough idea of the density of rock painting. In California and Texas, where intensive work has been done on the subject over a period of many years, the record is relatively complete. In such states as Wyoming and Montana, the work of recording sites has barely begun.

was the western boundary of the Great Plains. From north to south, I have drawn it along the main crest of the Rocky Mountains to an area slightly east of Santa Fe. From there it follows the Pecos River to its junction with the Rio Grande.

There are two basic styles of pictographs in western North America. One is the geometric or abstract. This type predominates on the Pacific Coast and in the Southwest. The other is the naturalistic and occurs mainly in the Great Plateau country and on the Great Plains. It is interesting that, with few ex-

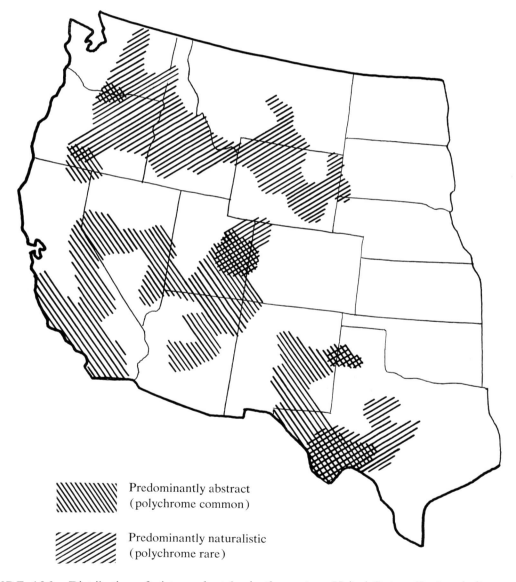

Predominantly abstract
(polychrome common)

Predominantly naturalistic
(polychrome rare)

FIGURE 106. Distribution of pictograph styles in the western United States. (Scattered sites east of the Mississippi are mainly naturalistic.) The abstract Chumash paintings follow the basic pattern of the areas to the north and east. Naturalistic paintings are dominant in the Great Plains and Columbia Plateau country.

ceptions, the creators of abstract paintings were the people living in permanent settlements. These were the fishing people, the food gatherers, and the primitive agriculturists. The naturalistic pictures were the work of the nomads and the hunters. Their pictographs run heavily to the larger game animals like the mountain sheep, the bison, and the elk. In addition, they often show hunters and warriors. Where the two ways of life overlapped, as in the Fremont culture of eastern Utah or in the southwest corner of Texas, this overlap shows up in the mixture of design elements.

In Canada, there are naturally extensions of the styles and techniques in the northern United States. Across southern Canada and particularly in the Canadian Shield region, great numbers of paintings are being recorded by Selwyn Dewdney (see Dewdney and Kidd, 1962). Alaska has a few pictographs, and these are the work of the Eskimos, especially around Kodiak Island and Cook Inlet. They are mainly naturalistic paintings in red, of sea and land mammals.

1. THE PACIFIC COAST

From the Canadian border to Baja California, the largest concentration of rock paintings is south and east of San Francisco. The following areas surround the Chumash.

Northeastern California. In the northeast counties of Siskiyou and Modoc, there are many pictograph sites. This is a country of extensive lava beds and the paintings are done on the smooth basaltic rocks. The designs are very simple, almost entirely abstract, with an occasional attempt to portray humans, insects, and suns. There is a little polychrome painting; the usual method is to use one color.

Monterey. Directly north of the arbitrary boundary of the Chumash country (according to Kroeber, the division was roughly the watershed between the Salinas and Santa Maria rivers), there are a few sites showing the same technique and design style as the Obispeño and southwestern California areas. The designs are very simple, usually geometric, and done in black or red.

From this section it is over fifty miles to the next pictograph zone in Monterey County. One large site here is reminiscent of the Tulare region (fig. 109a, c) with some polychrome painting, but other locations show quite simple designs in single colors. There is a concentration of eighteen sites in the Santa Lucia Mountains east of Point Sur. This is the furthest north that pictographs are found in coastal California.

Tulare. The second major concentration of pictographs in California is in the Sierra foothill region of Kern and Tulare counties. There is little sandstone here, and most of the paintings occur on the undersides of the immense granite boulders that are found throughout this region of oak and grassland. There are several large batholith intrusions in the Porterville–Exeter region, and the masses of tumbled rocks have formed many caves. In these areas there is an extraordinary number of paintings.

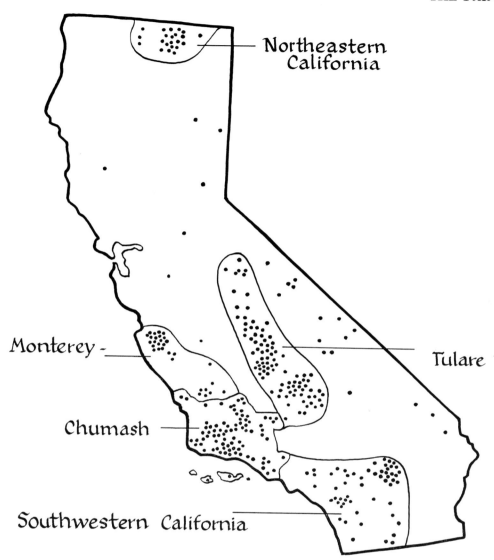

FIGURE 107. Pictograph sites in California. (Chumash area, Grant; other sites, Fenenga, 1949; unpublished material, Univ. of California; and J. J. Cawley, Bakersfield)

The general style is not unlike that of the Cuyama area. Elaborate polychrome designs are common. There are certain elements that are characteristic of the region, but the basic technique is close to that of the Chumash. There can be little doubt that there was much interchange of ideas across the broad San Joaquin Valley that divides the two pictograph zones. Most of the Tulare country was occupied by the Yokuts, who carried on extensive trade with the Chumash.

Southwestern California. Most of the sites in the six southern counties in California are found in San Diego and Riverside counties, from the coast ranges into the desert. The paintings are almost without exception done in single colors, 111

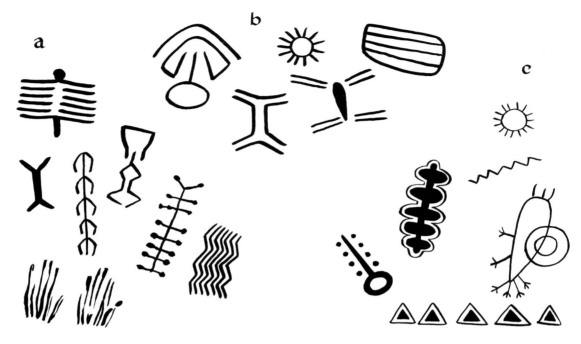

FIGURE 108.   Monterey and northeastern California design elements. a. Monterey County, some
in polychrome. Note similarity to Tulare pictographs. b. San Luis Obispo County (bordering
Chumash territory). All are in red. c. Northeastern California, occasionally in polychrome.
(Lowest a, and c, after Steward, 1929)

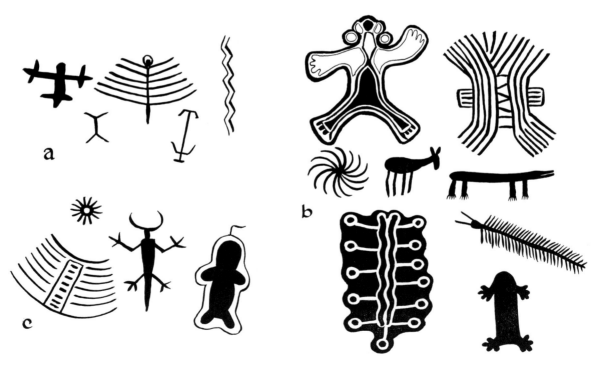

FIGURE 109.   Design elements from the Tulare region. a. North (Tulare County), red only. b. Central Tulare County, chiefly polychrome. c. South (Kern County), right figure in polychrome.

FIGURE 110. Southwestern California pictograph elements. The paintings with rare exceptions are in red. Note similarity of left pictographs to design elements from the Obispeño area (fig. 70). (After Steward, 1929)

usually red, and are painted on vertical surfaces of isolated boulders. The designs are simple—diamonds, dots, zigzags, wheels, and chevrons are the most common elements. They are very like the designs from the Obispeño area in the Chumash territory. We know that many of these were made in connection with girls' puberty rites (see p. 90).

2. GREAT BASIN

The Great Basin is an immense area of desert and semi-desert, embracing most of Nevada, half of Utah, and parts of California, Oregon, Idaho, and Wyoming. All streams flow inward to interior lakes or are dissipated in the desert sand.

The Great Basin painted style of Nevada and eastern California (see Heizer and Baumhoff, 1962) is very simple and crudely done. The color is almost invariably red with an occasional use of black, white, and yellow. The design elements are few, mostly nonrepresentational, with zigzags, circles, and parallel lines predominating. Some of these pictographs strongly resemble the simple puberty rite paintings of southwestern California. The petroglyphs of the same area (western and central Nevada and eastern California) show many animals, chiefly mountain sheep, none of which occur in the rock paintings. Heizer and Baumhoff suggest that these may have been made for magic-ceremonial reasons to bring good hunting. Their estimates on the petroglyphs go back as far as 5000 B.C., the pictographs from A.D. 1 to recent times.

113

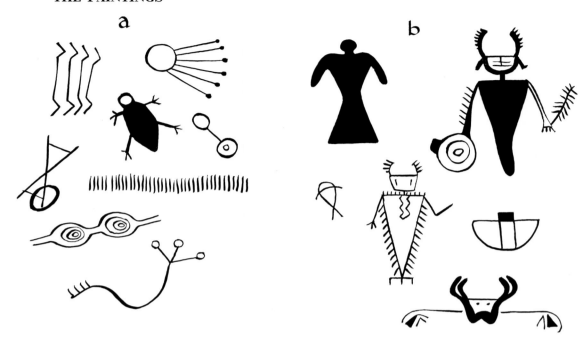

FIGURE 111.   Great Basin pictograph elements. a. Western and central Nevada, in red and black. b. Southeastern Nevada. (After Heizer and Baumhoff, 1962)

In southeastern Nevada they describe a number of sites as Puebloan painted, where square-shouldered kachina figures are common. The paintings are far more carefully done than the Great Basin painted designs to the west. These pictographs seem to be contemporaneous with Puebloid occupation of southeastern Nevada. This would place them between Basket Maker II (? to A.D. 500) and early Pueblo III (A.D. 1150).

3. SOUTHWEST

This country is dominated by the culture of the Pueblo people. Entering the Southwest in about A.D. 200 (see Gladwin, 1957), the ancestors of the present Pueblo Indians brought a knowledge of pottery, corn, and housebuilding. In about A.D. 1000, nomadic and warlike Indians began to move into the area from the north, wiping out settlements and forcing the concentration of the Pueblo people that developed the fortress type of architecture we know as Pueblo today. These northern marauders were certainly the Navajos and the Apaches.

At an early period, the Pueblo Indians had developed a strongly abstract style of design which can be seen today in their pottery designs, textiles, ceremonial costumes, and rock paintings. The nomadic tribes, unable to destroy the Pueblo people, stayed in the country and, along with their own hunting culture, adopted many Pueblo ideas, especially their style of design. The rock paintings in Arizona and New Mexico often depict the kachina figure, and many elements are reminiscent of pottery designs.

114   This influence extends into southeastern Nevada, southern and eastern Utah

(Fremont culture), Colorado, and southwestern Texas. There is much use of polychrome and the paintings are generally done with great care. The Navajos, under the influence of the Pueblos and especially after contact with Europeans, became excellent artists and craftsmen. They adapted and elaborated on many of the ceremonial practices of the Pueblos, including sand painting, and made striking pictographs in northern Arizona and New Mexico.

FIGURE 112.   Southwest pictograph elements. a. Navajo, Canyon de Chelly: left, red, yellow, and white; right, blue, white, and black. b. Pueblo: left, Frijoles Canyon, red; right, northeastern Arizona: red, yellow, white. c. Southwest Texas: left, red outlined with white; right, red. d. Fremont culture, eastern Utah: both red. e. Southern Utah: white. (a, from photographs by David Gebhard; b, after Kidder and Guernsey, 1919; c, after Jackson, 1938; d, left, after Morss, 1931; d, right, after Wormington, 1955; e, after Steward, 1941)

4. COLUMBIA PLATEAU

This northern region is bounded on the west by the Cascade Mountains and on the east by the Rockies. It is drained by the mighty Columbia River and its great tributary, the Snake. It is along these rivers and their innumerable feeder streams that most of the rock paintings are found. On the Columbia, the paintings, usually in red, are found near the fishing villages and on the basalt cliffs that border the semi-arid middle and upper reaches of the river.   115

Fishing, especially for the Pacific salmon, dominated the way of life of most of these people, although in the interior the nomadic tribes hunted for the larger game animals.

Some of the pictographs on the lower and middle Columbia show a marked Northwest coast abstract influence. Further inland the designs are mainly naturalistic, the usual style of roving bands of hunting Indians.

FIGURE 113. Columbia Plateau pictograph elements. a. Long Narrows of the mid-Columbia. The masklike design is pecked in the rock and painted red. The others are red and white. b. Upper Columbia and tributaries, central Washington. c. Columbia drainage, north central Oregon. d. Central Idaho. e. Harney–Malheur Basin, eastern Oregon. (a, after E. Strong, 1959; b, after Cain, 1950; c and e, after Cressman, 1937; d, after Erwin, 1930)

5. GREAT PLAINS

The name Great Plains conjures up endless vistas of prairie—the "sea of grass" of the books on western travel. This region—eventually the wheat and corn heartland of the country—provided few rocky areas to attract the Indian painter. The known pictographs are concentrated in the Rocky Mountain country to the west, thinning out or disappearing at the lower altitudes.

The Indians of the Great Plains were almost entirely nomadic hunting people, and the pictographs from this region are predominantly naturalistic. Large game animals are favorite subjects, with many representations of armed warriors and hunters. In the northern country there are examples of "shield" designs, either a round shape decorated with devices typical of the shields of the mounted Plains Indian warriors or curious anthropomorphic figures with shield-shaped bodies.

116

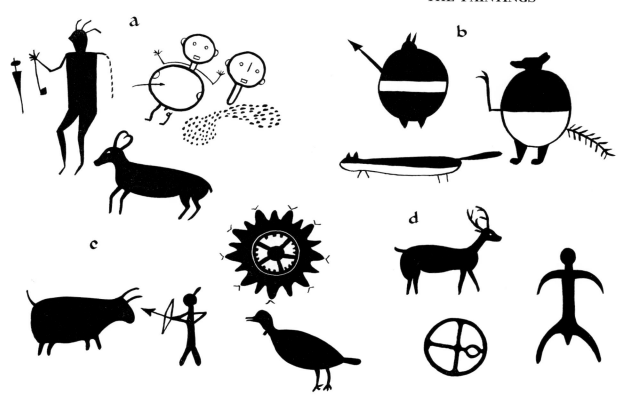

FIGURE 114.   Great Plains pictograph elements. All figures shown were done in red. a. Wyoming.
b. Montana. c. Central Texas. d. Eastern New Mexico. (a, left, and d, after Renaud, 1936;
a, right, from photograph by David Gebhard; b, after Secrist, 1960; c, after Jackson, 1938)

In central Texas numbers of sites have abstract designs mixed with naturalistic elements. An elaborate sun or shield design is shown in figure 114c. Red is the usual color in all Great Plains pictographs, with some black and white.

The drawing of animals reaches its most realistic point in the rock paintings of the Great Plains and the Eastern Woodland but never approaches the skill of the Palaeolithic artists of France and Spain.

6. EASTERN WOODLAND

The country east of the Mississippi is not a very rewarding one for the student of rock painting. Mallery in his great work on the picture writing of the North American Indians gives only four painted sites for the entire area. A recent count shows that the number is now twenty-nine. There are no known sites, either petroglyphs or pictographs, in the states of Connecticut, Delaware, Florida, Indiana, Louisiana, Mississippi, New Hampshire, and South Carolina (Tatum, 1946). This may be due to a lack of ideal painting surfaces in protected caves (the greater dampness and humidity of the east would destroy paintings in exposed spots) or to the fact that the Indians here simply had no tradition of rock art. In any case, rock carvings are rather common in some   117

FIGURE 115.   Eastern Woodland pictograph elements. a. Minnesota–Ontario border: red. b. Eastern Missouri: red. c. Brattleboro, Vermont: white. d. Southern Illinois: red and white. (*a*, re-
drawn from *Indian Rock Paintings of the Great Lakes* by Selwyn Dewdney and Kenneth E.
Kidd, published by University of Toronto Press, 1962; b, after Diesing and Magre, 1942;
c, after Willoughby, 1935; d, upper left, after McAdams, 1887; others, after Peithman, 1952)

eastern states but paintings are rare; even the anthropological literature is
scarce and fragmentary.

The most numerous paintings of which we have knowledge are the Ojibway
pictographs in the Minnesota–Ontario border area. Numbers of them are found
on granite cliffs bordering lakes and could only have been painted from a canoe.
The country where the Missouri and Ohio rivers join the Mississippi has a few
sites, one with a better-than-usual deer painting (fig. 115*b*). Most of the remaining sites are in the Tennessee Valley.

7. BAJA CALIFORNIA

The Jesuit missionaries who began their work on the peninsula in the late
1600's were the first to note the Indian rock paintings, but it was not until 1894
that the Frenchman Léon Diguet published his extensive investigations of the
Baja pictographs. The thirty sites he described were nearly all in the central
mountains, the Sierra Giganta, the Sierra de Santa Lucia, and the Sierra de San
Francisco.

The usual style features such design elements as zigzags, suns, and grids and is
done in the simple linear technique found in the adjoining southern California
area. There are two exceptions to this basic abstract style. On the southeast coast

118

near La Paz, there is a site featuring well-drawn animals and fish, the fish painted in a vertical position (fig. 116c). In the central and eastern part of the peninsula there is a region of palm-lined canyons, usually with water—that rarest of Baja resources—where Diguet described three extraordinary sites.

At each of these the caves or rock shelters were large, with great numbers of over-life-sized figures of men and animals and fish, often painted twenty or more feet from the ground. The human figures were often painted red and black with the colors divided longitudinally or horizontally on the body (fig. 116d). The fish were invariably painted in a vertical position, as in the site near La Paz.

In 1962, the writer Erle Stanley Gardner, on an exploring trip into this region of "giant figure" painting, found a fourth example of this curious style. His site is very large, including several caves and over a hundred individual figures—men, mountain sheep, deer, whales, and rabbits. A radiocarbon age of plus 500 years was obtained from a wooden artifact in the main cave.

The intrusion into central Baja of this very distinctive pictograph style is intriguing and suggests a migration down the coast or across the gulf of California by a nomadic hunting people attracted to the area by the available water and abundant large game animals.

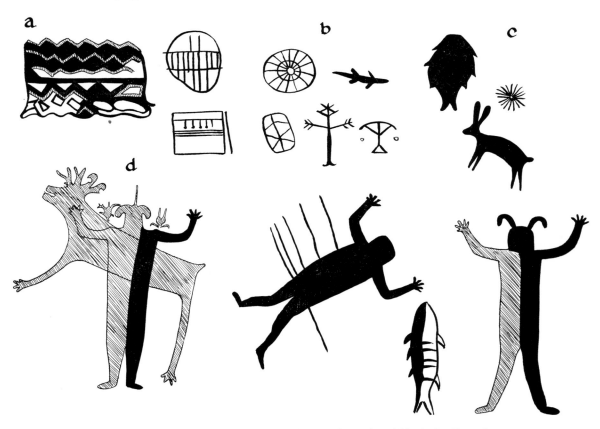

FIGURE 116. Baja California pictograph elements. a. Northern Baja: red and black. b. Central Baja: red. c. Southern Baja: red or black. d. "Giant figure" area of central Baja: red and black. (a, after Steward, 1929; b, c, and d [middle and right], after Diguet, 1894; d, left, after Gardner, 1962b)

119

THE PAINTINGS

Europe

In the summer of 1879, the small daughter of the amateur archaeologist, Marcelino de Sautola, discovered the celebrated bison paintings in the cave at Altamira in northern Spain, and the study of early rock painting began. These paintings are the work of late Palaeolithic man and were probably made in connection with hunting-magic ceremonies to bring good fortune in the hunt. No finer animal drawings have ever been made.

FIGURE 117. European cave paintings. a. Southern France. Right and left, Font-de-Gaume: red; center, Lascaux: black. b. Northern Spain. Left, cave near Oviedo: brown; right, Castillo cave: red; lower, Altamira: polychrome. c. Eastern Spain. (a, left and right, from Graziosi, 1960, after Breuil; b, after Graziosi, 1960; c, after Obermaier and Weinert, 1919)

After the Altamira discovery, many more caves were located, the richest finds being in the Dordogne, in the valley of the Vézère, the Pyrenees, and in eastern Spain. The French and northern Spanish paintings are almost without exception of animals, many of long-extinct ice age mammals, reflecting man's complete dependence on hunting at that time. The cave of Lascaux, found above the Vézère Valley in 1940, is the most spectacular of Palaeolithic sites, with many galleries of paintings in excellent condition. The earliest of the European paintings may be nearly 30,000 years old.

The paintings from eastern Spain seem much later and here the emphasis, though still on hunting, often features the hunter. The many figures of men,

120

shooting the bow, running, and dancing, are filled with life and are wonderfully well done. The resemblance between these paintings and some of those from north Africa is striking.

Africa

There has been a great interest over a long period of time in the rock paintings of Africa, and an infinite number of them have been recorded and reproduced. From the Tassili paintings in the Sahara south across the vast continent to Capetown, there is the most amazing homogeneity. The creators of the paintings were hunters, herdsmen, and primitive agriculturists. From all areas, the basic themes are people and animals, and these are superbly done. There is little abstract work, and most of it is rather crudely done.

The Tassili pictographs are the most diverse and fascinating of all African rock art. This vast treasury of prehistoric art was described by Henri Lhote in 1958. He illustrated a number of styles, many having a close affinity with eastern Spain and with central and southern Africa, while others feature giant anthropomorphic figures not unlike the oversized figures from central Baja California.

FIGURE 118.   African pictographs. a. North Africa. Tassili region of the Sahara: elements of different periods, polychrome. b. Central and south Africa: upper left, northern Rhodesia; eland and warrior, southern Rhodesia; c. kudu, southern Rhodesia; dancing figures, Union of South Africa, southeast coast. All paintings in monochrome. (a, after Lhote, 1959; b, after Goodall, Cooke, and Clark, 1959; c, after Burkitt, 1928)

121

Some show a strong Egyptian influence in the conventionalized human figure; some picture chariots. It is evident from the many styles and overpainting that a long span of time was involved.

The age of African rock art has been estimated to have extended from 7,000 years ago down to the early 1800's (Bandi, 1961).

Australia

The continent of Australia is rich in rock paintings, both ancient and modern. In the areas where the native culture is relatively undisturbed, pictographs are still being painted and here we can learn something of their purpose.

The most interesting rock art is the *wondjina* painting in northwestern Australia. These curious anthropomorphic figures are invariably painted without mouths, sometimes with bodies and sometimes without. The paintings are repainted every year just before the rains by the chief whose tribe owes its beginnings to that particular *wondjina*. This gives renewed strength to the *wondjina*, who is the bringer of rain and normal increase of all living things. Some paintings are used in fertility ceremonies and others are clan totemic figures.

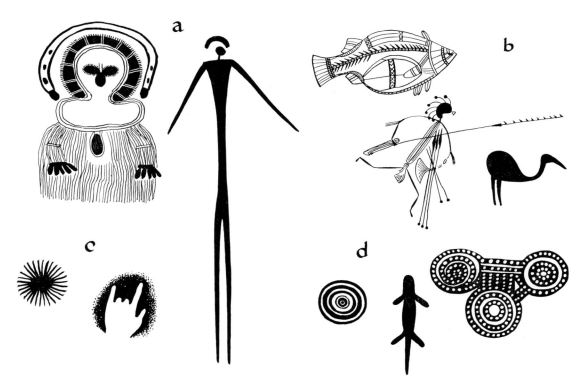

FIGURE 119.   Australian pictographs. a. Northwestern Australia. Left, *Wondjina* painting, Kimberley District: red, white, and black; right, elegant style figure, Wonalirri: red. b. Northern Australia. Fish and man from Oenpelli; curlew in white, Wardman tribe. c. Southeast Australia. d. Central Australia: design at right in red, white, and black. (a, left, b, right, and c, after Davidson, 1936; a, right, and b, upper left, from Bandi, 1961; b, lower left, from Bandi, 1961, after Mountford, 1956; d, from Davidson, 1936, after Stirling, 1896)

Also in northwest Australia are found curiously attenuated figures in the so-called "elegant style." They are older than the *wondjina* paintings and do not seem to have had a ceremonial purpose.

Animal forms predominate in the north and southwest, while abstract forms are found in the center of the continent, where there are many geometric designs, some done with dotted lines in a manner reminiscent of the Chumash paintings. These are the closest in style and technique to the Santa Barbara and Tulare areas of any known pictographs. The hand stencil is common in Australia, often showing one or more amputated fingers, evidence of some curiously senseless rite. The most extraordinary paintings are found at Oenpelli, northern Australia. Here creatures, especially fish, are done in an X-ray style showing the internal organs. Human figures reduced to spidery semiabstractions run about with fantastically long spears and spear throwers.

The age of Australian painting has been placed from a possible 4,000 B.C. to the present (Bandi, 1961).

There are many other areas in the world where pictographs occur and there are publications on some of these, including Siberia, Alaska, British Columbia, South America, and the Caribbean. In this chapter, I have had to limit myself to the better known regions.

Conclusions

For many years it was generally accepted that the pictographs in the Santa Barbara area were the work of the Chumash, but direct evidence was scanty. The evidence has been accumulating, however, especially in the last few years, and the case for the Chumash artists begins to look very good indeed.

The Chumash–Canaliño culture of the coast seems almost identical with excavated sites in the interior. The Alamo Pintado site (Deetz, 1964), the James–Abels collection from the Cuyama (now at the Santa Barbara Museum of Natural History), and the explorations in northeastern Santa Barbara County (Strong, 1935) all show a Canaliño culture. These sites are all close to pictograph caves.

This seems to put our painters in the right places, but what about the time element? Radiocarbon dating gives us a good starting clue. An early Canaliño site on Santa Rosa Island has been dated at 2,950 years ago (Orr, 1956). A radiocarbon test on pigment from a Santa Barbara area pictograph site showed that the sample was "not over 2,000 years old." Fragments of a basket found in a cave cache within a few hundred feet of a painted cave were dated by radiocarbon at 120 years plus or minus 80 years. With the James–Abels Canaliño burial artifacts from the Cuyama are many trade beads and other Spanish contact material. Here again is late material near painted sites.

There are two recent articles on pictographs in association with late prehistoric and historic artifacts. Deetz *A Dateable Chumash Pictograph From Santa*   123

Barbara County (1964) describes a typical pictograph on a detached rock found with contact material at the Alamo Pintado site. Eberhart and Babcock (1963) describe projectile points found near pictograph site V-1 as typical of late Santa Barbara coastal and San Joaquin. Another clue is that, though the early explorers in the Santa Barbara area made no mention of rock painting, they noted abstract designs painted on burial markers in the coastal cemeteries. As additional evidence that the practice of rock painting persisted until early Spanish times in some areas, there is the pictograph (pl. 26) showing four horsemen. The rate of erosion demonstrated by a set of rock pictures recorded by Mallery in the 1890's and now scarcely visible would indicate no great age for some paintings, though in other instances overpainting and the amount of patination over the pigment suggest that the practice of making these pictures was carried on over a long period. I think that a time span from about 1,000 years ago down to the beginning of the mission period would not be unreasonable.

I have attempted to gather together the story of the Chumash Indians from many widely scattered references. They were the first Indians in California to come into close contact with Europeans. All the explorers spoke of their high culture and gentleness. Unable to survive the enforced contact with the Spanish under the mission system, they and their culture died, leaving the investigator with many unanswered questions. None is more fascinating or provocative than the riddle of the rock paintings. It seems certain that most of them were painted by the shamans for magic or ceremonial reasons, although some may have been in the nature of a recording or special marking of a site.

A study of design elements across the United States shows an interesting pattern. Abstract painting dominates in areas of settled community life. In regions populated by roving bands of hunting people, the paintings run heavily to naturalistic forms—large game animals, hunters, and warriors. This pattern can be traced in the other great pictograph areas of the world. The beautifully painted animals of Palaeolithic man in Europe were the product of a culture completely dependent on hunting. The paintings in Africa are almost without exception of game animals and hunters. In Australia, the pattern is mixed; some areas, such as central and southern Australia, run heavily to the abstract, while others feature the larger game marsupials, fish, and hunters.

The predominance of abstract pictographs in areas of permanent village life points to another consideration. It is likely that much primitive design starts with an attempt at naturalism, becoming increasingly formalized as the tradition continues until in long-established community areas the patterns become so abstract as to be almost unrecognizable by an outsider. A good example of this is the extraordinary stylized design of the Northwest Indians from the Columbia to southern Alaska. Here animals, birds, and fish are so reduced to pure pattern that the untrained observer can see no resemblance to natural forms.

The map (fig. 105) seems to indicate a pattern. The peoples of the Pacific coast and the Southwest may have arrived from Asia at a relatively early period, passing through a purely hunting phase into a food-gathering and primitive agricultural type of existence featured by permanent settlements. During this change,

124

the paintings associated with ceremonies went through a stylization from naturalistic to abstract. The later nomadic people entering the land to the east of the Cascades were still in a hunting culture and were painting chiefly hunting pictures when they were overwhelmed by the whites who had given up hunting and food gathering as a way of life several thousands of years earlier. The abstract tradition may have been developed independently in California or it may have been a diffusion from the Southwest. Ground paintings in southern California associated with puberty rites are certainly an imported idea from the Arizona–New Mexico country. That there was some trade between the areas was noted by one of the explorers, who saw a Southwest type of blanket in a Chumash village. Many seashells have been found in Southwest sites.

Of the major pictograph regions of the world, only one, central Australia, has paintings resembling the abstract polychromes of the Chumash country. The use of dots to pick out a design and the outlining of figures in another color are common techniques in both areas.

In all human societies where an art tradition has been established, there occasionally appears an especially gifted person, who while working with the known styles produces work far superior in design and execution to anything previously done in his country. Sometimes such a person is able to establish a school or a new tradition. The potter Maria of San Ildefonso Pueblo in New Mexico is such an artist. The steatite whale figure in figure 60 and the superb pictograph in the San Emigdio area (pl. 27) were the creations of first-rate artists. As the latter is the sole example of this elaborate style, we can only suppose that others may still be undiscovered in the mountains or that for some reason the painter did only one picture. He may have been killed in a hunting accident, shot by *gringo* settlers, or taken off to a mission to spend his days making adobe bricks.

It seems clear that the Chumash paintings followed a recognizable Stone Age man pattern. Though we can never hope to know very much about the meaning of their paintings, we can enjoy looking at them. The curious combinations of form and color are a constant delight to the eye. As Sigurd Olsen, a past president of the National Parks Association, put it:

> The primitive paintings on our cliff faces and all over the world are evidences of man's first reaching out for meaning and expression. Wherever they are found, they are symbols of his eternal striving, shrines for the mind and spirit of man.

APPENDIXES

APPENDIX A

San Nicolás Island

South and southeast of the Santa Barbara Channel Islands are four more islands. The three largest are Santa Catalina, San Clemente, and San Nicolás, all of which had permanent settlements. The smallest, Santa Barbara Island, was used intermittently, probably as a fishing camp. All of these islands were in the territory of the Shoshonean-speaking Gabrieliño.

San Nicolás lies about 65 miles from the nearest shore and has been a source of very fine artifacts, perhaps the finest that have been taken from the Chumash–Gabrieliño region.

All we know of the culture of the historic San Nicolás islanders comes from the accounts of the lost woman of San Nicolás, a Crusoe-like tale of an Indian woman, abandoned for eighteen years on the island. As the story includes the only detailed eye-witness account of the way of life of a Channel Island Indian, it is worth retelling.

In 1811, a Boston trading vessel took a party of Kodiak Indians from Sitka in Russian America to San Nicolás to hunt otter. They were left on the island for a period of months while the ship went south to Baja California. There was fighting with the native islanders over the women, and many men were killed by the Kodiaks. When the otter hunters were picked up by their ship, all contact with the island was broken for twenty-four years.

In 1835, a schooner with the unhappy name of *Peor es Nada* ("Worse Than Nothing") sailed from Santa Barbara on an otter hunt in Baja California.   129

FIGURE 120.
Petroglyphs of killer whales from a cave on San Nicolás Island. (After Reinman and Townsend, 1960)

Aboard was a trapper from the Rocky Mountains named Bill Williams.[1] Three months later the crew put in at San Pedro and were given a special job by the local missionaries. The Franciscans were scraping the bottom of the heathen barrel, and the church decided to remove the remnants of the San Nicolás islanders to the mainland. The *Peor es Nada* sailed for San Nicolás with instructions to round up all Indians and bring them back to San Pedro.

This turned out to be a simple enough job. Between the Kodiak massacre and the diseases left by otter hunters, there were only eighteen Indians left. One, a young woman, was left behind because she had gone looking for her child. Due to the stormy weather, the schooner could not wait for her and sailed for the mainland. The "rescued" Indians were sent to Los Angeles and Mission San Gabriel. It was the intention to send the ship back to pick up the missing woman, but the *Peor es Nada* was sunk soon after, and no attempt was made to look for her until 1850. That year a search was made on San Nicolás for the woman. No trace of her was found and all thought of further search was abandoned. In 1852, George Nidever, a fur trapper who had come to California with the famous Walker exploration party in 1833, sailed to San Nicolás with an Indian crew to look for sea-gull eggs, which were in great demand locally. They saw fresh footprints near some brush huts but before they could carry out a search, one of the savage northwesters hit them. After eight days of storm, they sailed for the mainland and reported signs of the missing Indian.

[1]There is a possibility this may have been the almost legendary mountain man, Bill Williams. In 1833 Joseph Reddeford Walker was sent by Captain Bonneville to explore the country to the west of the Great Salt Lake. With him went a party of over forty seasoned trappers including Alexis Godey, Bill Williams, Zenas Leonard, George Nidever, and Joe Meek. The party reached California, discovering the Yosemite Valley on the way, and wintered at Monterey. Most of these men returned to the Rockies but several, including Nidever, stayed in California. It is known that Williams and others returned to California on a number of occasions, attracted by the ease of horse stealing from the big ranchos and missions. In writing of the Bill Williams who went with the *Peor es Nada* to San Nicolás, Nidever wrote, "I remember distinctly . . . a man named Williams, a former acquaintance of mine in the Rocky Mountains. . . . Williams of the Chino Ranch in Los Angeles County, and who was with me in the Mts., he with Col. Bean having shown the white feather in our first engagement with the Indians on the Ark. River. He afterwards took one of the Indian women [from San Nicolás] to live with."

The following winter, Nidever returned to San Nicolás to hunt otter. He had instructions from Father Gonzales to make every effort to find the woman. Soon after landing, they again saw fresh footprints in the sand and numbers of wild dogs. In a bush, they found a basket, covered with a piece of seal skin. In the basket were several bird skins, cut square, a long twisted sinew rope and some bone needles. They spread the contents around on the ground with the intention of seeing if they were replaced at a later visit. Again a storm came up and they returned to Santa Barbara.

The next spring, Nidever sailed for San Nicolás, prepared to stay several months. They found a good spring near the western end of the island with human footprints around it. They relocated the basket and found that it had been refilled with its contents and hung on a bush. By following the footprints, the woman was seen near some huts made of whale ribs and brush. She was stripping blubber from a piece of sealskin as she watched the hunters closing in on her. She showed no sign of fear and chattered away at the Chumash crewmen in an unintelligible language. After a while she roasted some roots on the fire in the shelter and offered them to her visitors. Blubber was drying on stakes and suspended from sinew ropes. There were a number of baskets nearby, some in various stages of manufacture, and two bottle-shaped water baskets. Other articles were fishhooks and needles of bone, fishing lines of sinew, and a large rope for snaring sleeping seals.

The woman was about 50 years of age, of medium height and rather stocky. Her dress was made of cormorant skins, sleeveless, tied at the waist with a cord and reaching to the ground. She indicated that during the rainy season she lived in a nearby cave. Nidever, by sign language, told the woman they had come to take her away, and she at once packed up her belongings in baskets, including a very ripe seal's head, and followed the men to a spring near shore where her things were left. She was then taken aboard the schooner and given a meal of hardtack and beans, which she ate with relish.

The following day, the otter hunters set up a camp near the middle of the island and the Indian woman kept the camp supplied with wood and with water, which she carried in her water baskets. Nidever saw her lining such a water basket one day:

> She had built a fire and had several small stones about the size of a walnut heating in it. Taking one of the vessels, which was in shape and size very like a demijohn, excepting that the neck and mouth were much longer, she dropped a few pieces of asphaltum within it and as soon as the stones were well heated they were dropped in on top of the asphaltum. They soon melted it, when, resting the bottom of the vessel on the ground, she gave it a rotary motion with both hands until the interior was completely covered with asphaltum.

About a month later the Indian woman was brought back to Santa Barbara and lived with the Nidevers. She was immensely good-humored and spent much time singing and dancing. Many people came to see the famous "lost woman," and attempts were made to understand her language but with no success. The few words that were recorded are *to-co*, a hide; *na-che*, a man; *te-gua*, the sky;   131 and *pinche*, the body. On the basis of these four words, Kroeber stated that the San Nicolás islanders spoke a Shoshonean dialect.[2]

The abrupt change of diet from dried seal blubber to the rich and varied Santa Barbara foods proved too much for the Indian woman. She became very weak and, within seven weeks, was dead. The Mission padres were content, however; she had been baptized Juana Maria.

[2]Bleak, deserted San Nicolás Island is deserted no longer. The U. S. Navy has taken over the island and built a large missile tracking station, doubtless destroying much prehistoric material in the construction of airfields and elaborate military installations. The inevitable scrawled and carved names are appearing in the cave of the killer whales.

APPENDIX B

Chinigchinich

Father Gerónimo Boscana, Franciscan friar at San Juan Capistrano Mission from May, 1814 to January, 1826, was unique among the devout men of the California mission system. He faithfully carried out his share in the great work of saving pagan souls, but was intensely interested in the customs, religion, and traditions of the local Indians, the Juaneño. He justified his curiosity by saying that it was difficult to eliminate heathen beliefs without understanding them.

The manuscript of his study of the Juaneño was found in the archives of the Santa Barbara Mission by Alfred Robinson, an early resident who translated it into English and published the account in his *Life in California* in 1846. According to Kroeber, Father Boscana's memoir is "easily the most intensive and best written account of the customs and religion of any group of California Indians in the mission days."

Some excerpts follow:

> All their knowledge is from tradition which they preserve in songs for their dances, and these are introduced by the chief at their festivities in a language distinct from that in common use. Others unite with them but without understanding the meaning of what they do or articulate . . .
>
> An invisible and all-powerful being called Nocuma made the world, the sea, and all that is therein contained, such as animals, trees, plants and fishes. In form it was spherical, and rested on his hands. By being continually in motion, he resolved to secure the world by placing in its center a black rock called Tosaut, and it remained firm and secure as at the present time.
>
> Nocuma, having created all the things contained in the world . . . created man, or the first Indian, out of the earth and called him Ejoni. Afterwards he created

133

woman and gave her the name of Ae. Many years after the creation of Ejoni and Ae, one of their descendants called Sirout and his wife, called Ycaiut, had a son, and they gave him the name of Ouiot. At that time, all the inhabitants were at peace, and quietly following their domestic pursuits, but Ouiot, being of a fierce disposition, a warrior ambitious and haughty, soon managed to gain a supremacy over many of the towns . . . he gradually exposed his ferocity and persecuted many of his vassals, treating them cruelly and some he put to death.

Having suffered so much from Ouiot, they determined to rid themselves of the tyrant . . . by means of poison. One of them was trusted with its execution and at night finding Ouiot asleep, placed a small quantity (of poison) on his breast. On waking, he experienced a sickness and weakness in his limbs . . . until at length he died.

Many years, and perhaps ages, having expired since the death of Ouiot, there appeared in the same town of Pubuna, one called Ouiamot. And this was the god Chingchinich, so feared, venerated, and respected by the Indians, who taught first in the town of Pubuna, and afterward in all the neighboring parts, explaining the laws and establishing the rites and ceremonies necessary to the preservation of life.

One day at a very large congregation of the people, he danced before them, adorned in the robes that have already been described (a feathered dress), with his flesh painted black and red, and calling himself Tobet. He said he had come from the stars to teach them those things of which they were ignorant. After dancing a considerable time, he separated the chiefs and elders from among them, and directed that they alone should wear the kind of dress which had adorned his person, and taught them how to dance. To these Indians was given the name of *puplem*, who would know all things, and relieve the infirm and diseased. In other words, they would become the sorcerers or soothsayers, to whom the Indian might invariably apply for advice and relief from their necessities. . . . (he) taught them how to build the *vanquech*, which means "temple" or "church" and how they were to conduct themselves therein—forbidding any others than the chief and *puplem* entering the sanctuary.

The most celebrated of their feasts, which was observed yearly, was the one called *panes*, signifying a bird feast. The Indians exhibited a particular adoration for a bird resembling much in appearance the common buzzard or vulture but of larger dimensions [California condor]. . . . on the opening of the festival, they carried the *panes* in solemn procession, and placed it on the altar erected for the purpose. Then immediately, all the young married and unmarried females commenced running to and fro with great rapidity, some in one direction and some in another, more like distracted than rational beings. . . . The *puplem*, painted . . . and looking like so many devils, in the meantime danced around their adored *panes*.

These ceremonies being concluded, they seized upon the bird and carried it in procession to the principal *vanquech*, or temple. . . . Arriving at the temple, they killed the bird without losing a particle of its blood. The skin was removed entire, and preserved with the feathers as a relic. . . . The carcase was interred within the temple in a hole previously prepared, around which all the old women soon collected. While weeping and moaning most bitterly, the latter kept throwing upon the dead bird various kinds of seeds or particles of food and exclaiming at the same time, "Why did you run away? Would you not have been better with us? You would have made *pinole* as we do, and if you had not run away you would not have become a *panes*. . . . as ceremony was concluding, the dancing commenced again, and continued for three days and nights. . . . The Indians state

134

that the *panes* was once a female who ran off and retired to the mountains. Accidentally meeting with Chinigchinich, he changed her into a bird. . . .

The ancients said that when an Indian died, though the body was burnt, still the heart was not consumed . . . and that it went to a place destined by Chinigchinich. If a chief or one of the *puplem*, it went to dwell among the stars, and like them threw its light upon the earth. Others who were not of noble rank, were doomed to the borders of the sea, or to the hills, mountains, valleys or forests. There they remained an indefinite time while Chinigchinich made them do penance. . . .

I have quoted at length from this interesting account (Robinson, *op. cit.*, pp. 236–341) as it gives a very good picture of typical California Indian religious beliefs and practices. The worship of Chinigchinich centered in the Gabrieliño country and possibly spread to adjoining parts of the Chumash area.

APPENDIX C

The Radiocarbon Method of Dating

In 1951, Dr. Willard Libby published his pioneer work on radiocarbon dating. Since that time thousands of ancient specimens have been dated through this revolutionary process.

Carbon 14 is a radioactive isotope of carbon with an atomic weight of 14 instead of the normal 12. It is formed in the atmosphere by bombardment of nitrogen atoms by cosmic rays. All living things, animal and vegetable, absorb *carbon 14* at a constant rate. At death, this absorption stops and the *carbon 14* begins to decay at a known and steady rate. It has been determined that half the radioactive carbon in a given sample will be left after about 5,570 years. The sample is purified and processed through apparatus that filters out background radiation. The amount of *carbon 14* is then determined by a Geiger counter technique, the number of clicks determining the remaining amount of radioactive material. From this the date at which the sample ceased to live can be stated with considerable accuracy.

The method allows for a margin of error in each direction, and radiocarbon dates are often written like this: 2590 B.P. (before present) ± 360 years; in other words, the sample might be 360 years older or 360 years younger than the B.P. date. In a dating of a cave basket, my guess was that the basket might be anywhere from 150 to 200 years old. The laboratory gave a dating of 120 B.P. ± 80 years, a confirmation of the postulated date.

136

APPENDIX D

Léon de Cessac, Early Investigator of the Chumash

Until recently (Reichlen and Heizer, 1963), the curious story of Léon de Cessac's expedition to California had not been told. Our only knowledge was from a few brief reports published in France in the 1880's and a paragraph in Rogers' *Prehistoric Man of the Santa Barbara Coast* (1929).

The expedition as planned and approved by the Department of Public Instruction was to be financed by the other member of the party, Alphonse Pinart, who had inherited a considerable fortune. The Government support consisted of a small subsidy for Cessac, a scientist previously known for his studies of soil and volcanic phenomena. Pinart preceded Cessac to the Americas and was reunited briefly with his collaborator in Lima, Peru, early in 1877 and then left for a long trip through Oceania. Cessac, after finishing his Peruvian collecting, was taken to California on a French frigate.

In San Francisco, Cessac accepted an invitation from the French wool company operating on Santa Cruz Island to conduct an archaeological investigation there. Excited over his finds, Cessac hired a schooner and extended his collecting to include the islands of Anacapa, Santa Rosa, San Miguel, and San Nicolás and the mainland. The great cemeteries of the islands and the Santa Barbara coast were, with few exceptions, untouched at this time and Cessac put together a collection of over 4,000 specimens. It was during his mainland collecting that he ran into the difficulties with the rival collector Paul Schumacher, described in the text.

In July, 1878, Pinart arrived in Santa Barbara from France and broke the news to Cessac that he was bankrupt, that the mission was ended, and that there would be no further financial help. Unfortunately the trusting archaeologist had borrowed large sums from businessmen and French friends and had only his small subsidy to continue with. He made a trip to some of the northern missions with Pinart, who was collecting Indian vocabularies, and then settled for a time in San Luis Obispo with his collections at the home of some French friends who still gave him credit.

For another year, Cessac worked in the Chumash territory, taking down vocabularies, photographing ethnic types, and studying the religious practices of the Santa Ynez area. He returned to France, but stored his ethnic material and field notes with a Mr. Dallidet in San Luis Obispo.

In Paris he tried to obtain financial assistance from the government to cover his Californian debts but without success. Badgered by lawyers and threatened with police action, the unfortunate Cessac was forced to change his lodgings often. During this time he devoted himself to organizing and writing his California material, which included over a hundred steel-engraved plates and many drawings on the island archaeology.

In September or October, 1881, Cessac disappeared from his hotel, abandoning all his archaeological material and leaving a considerable new debt. For a long time he was thought dead, but ten years later it was discovered that he had fled to the south of France, giving up completely all scientific work and devoting himself to poetry and political pamphleteering. He died in February, 1891. His manuscripts, drawings, and photographs came into the hands of Dr. Hamy, director of the Ethnographic Museum of the Trocadero. It is known that all this irreplaceable material was still in Dr. Hamy's hands in 1898, but all have now disappeared except the priceless Boscana account of the Capistrano Indians. Why Hamy withheld this material and what became of it may never be known. To complete the sad tale, all the collections left in San Luis Obispo have vanished without a trace. Happily, the large archaeological collection Cessac abandoned at the hotel is now at the Musée de l'Homme in Paris and will be described in a forthcoming publication by Robert F. Heizer.

APPENDIX E

Mission Trade
with Mexico

A good idea of the economics of running a frontier mission can be gleaned from the letters of Father José Señán of the mission Buenaventura (Simpson, 1962).

The basic products processed for shipment to Mexico were hides, tallow, hemp, and sometimes otter skins. With the credit from the sale of these products, Señán would order manufactured goods and medicines from Mexico. In the early years of the mission, the annual supply ships from San Blas maintained the thread of communications with Mexico, but after 1810, with the start of the Wars of Independence, trade virtually ceased. In addition to supplies, the San Blas ships brought pay for the soldiers, mail, occasional replacements of priests and soldiers, and precious scraps of information about the outside world. From 1815 to 1820, the San Buenaventura mission received nothing from Mexico, and thereafter only an occasional Mexican or Peruvian trading ship visited the mission.

Here is Señán's order list for 1807 (Simpson, pp. 25-27):

> List of supplies ordered from Mexico by this Mission of the Seraphic Doctor San Buenaventura, for this year of 1708 [1807].
>
> 1   bbl. sacramental wine
> 1½   *arrobas* refined wax; 1 1-lb. Easter candle
> 6   bolts coarse blue flannel
> 400   *varas* striped sackcloth
> 30   lengths black skirting

12	bolts wide white blanket stuff; 3 bolts same, striped
10	bolts same, narrow; 15 bolts Villalta cloth
2	habits; 4 cowls; 4 tunics, with cords
1	bolt brabant; 6 small silk snuff handkerchiefs
1	white hat for Father Vitoria, like those worn at the College
4	*arrobas* superior chocolate; 4 *arrobas* fine chocolate; 3 *arrobas* ordinary chocolate
1	jar snuff [in margin: 3 lbs.]; 10 twists tobacco
14	lbs. candlewick
8	lbs. raw maguey fiber
14	lbs. spun maguey fiber, blue and white
12	plowshares
12	*arrobas* strap iron
4	Biscayan axes
6	hinges, 1 span wide
1,000	nails *de barrote* and *medio barrote*
1,000	tacks for carding combs
300	nails *de escora*; 300 *de media escora*
2	skimmers for the kitchen; 2 tin markers; 12 larding needles
2	handsaws
4	Puebla machetes
2	doz. Flemish sheath knives
1	large kettle
2	ladles
1	*arroba* raw anise seed; ½ *arroba* hard candy
1½	*arrobas* vermicelli
6	lbs. almonds
6	oz. cinnamon; 4 oz. saffron
4	lbs. pepper; 2 lbs. cloves; 2 doz. nutmegs
6	fine flour sifters
2	wire sieves; 2 same, of bristle
6	small glass bottles
1	*tompeate* anise; 1 of oregano; 1 of cumin; 1 of lavender
4	oz. *calaguala*; 6 lbs. *canafistula*
2	lbs. licorice lozenges
4	bottles syrup of citron; 1 phial distilled rosemary water
8	lbs. almond oil
4	bottles rose vinegar
1	bottle Catholic balsam
1	bottle *copaiba* oil
1	lb. althea ointment; 1 lb. Ysis ointment
1	lb. hernia plaster
2	oz. cream of tartar
2,000	*cabalongas*
½	*arroba* Puebla herb
12	strings blue glass beads; 2 strings large red transparent garnets; 2 strings small carnelians
2	bars Puebla soap
6	papers cobbler's needles; 1 doz. fine dressmaker's scissors
2,000	glass rings for heavy cords
1	bundle tinder
3	pieces carmine

 12 hanks Campeche twine; 12 hanks hemp twine
  1 lb. *munequilla* yarn; 1 lb. same, *de numeros*
 25 rolls Barcelona lace, a little more than a finger wide; 25 rolls same, three
      fingers wide
  1 gross corks
  2 bolts wide Brittany cloth, fine, genuine
  1 gross rockets; 12 pinwheels
  ½ *arroba* brazilwood
  1 *arroba* indigo
  1 painting of our Lord St. Roque, 1½ *varas* tall, well executed, in a gilded
      frame of split bamboo
  1 carved figure of Prince St. Michael Archangel, 1¾ *varas* tall
  1 consecrated altar table
  3 lecterns for altars
  2 altar tables, Italian or Roman style, ordinary height, painted in imitation
      jasper; sides and ends gilded
  1 Holy Crucifix for the altar, ¾ *vara* high, including base
  1 painting of the Via Crucis, well executed, oblong, 1½ *varas* wide and
      1 *vara* high; gilded frame
 25 *varas* fine white linen; 25 *varas* linen for covers
  6 lbs. tin; 6 lbs. lead
  2 pieces fine colored paper
100 sheets paper, all colors
  1 assortment iron wire, fine to coarse
  ¼ bolt blue Queretaro cloth
  2 doz. ordinary black hats
  1 ream fine paper, quarto, for letters
  2 pairs concave glasses, for tired eyes

FRAY JOSÉ SEÑÁN
FRAY MARCOS ANTONIO DE VITORIA

Mission San Buenaventura, March 4, 1807

[Added in postscript:]
1 Holy Crucifix
1 coffeepot

Bibliography

ANDERSON, E. N., JR.

1964 *A Bibliography of the Chumash and Their Predecessors.* University of California Archaeological Survey, no. 61. Berkeley.

ANGEL, MYRON

1910 *La Piedra Pintada.* Grafton Publishing Co., Los Angeles.

ANONYMOUS

1946 More steatite objects. *Southwest Museum Masterkey,* 20: 174. Los Angeles.

1947 *Southwest Museum Masterkey,* 21: 104. (Illustrations of steatite carvings.)

ARMSTRONG, A. L.

1936 A Bullroarer of Le Moustier Age from Pin Hole Cave, Cresswell Crags, *Derbyshire. Proceedings Prehistoric Society East Anglia,* 6: 330–34.

ASCENSIÓN, FATHER.

See Bolton (1925).

BANCROFT, H. H.

1883 *Native Races of the Pacific Coast,* vol. 1. Longmans, Green, London.

BANDI, H. G., *et al.*

1961 *The Art of the Stone Age.* Crown, New York.

BARTLETT, J. R.

1854 *Personal Narrative of Explorations in Texas, New Mexico, California, Sonora and Chihuahua.* Appleton, New York.

BLACKBURN, T.

1963 *A Manuscript Account of the Ventureño Chumash.* University of California Archaeological Survey Annual Report, 1962–1963. Los Angeles, pp. 135–160.

BOAS, F.

1927 *Primitive Art.* Harvard University Press, Cambridge, Mass.

BOLTON, H. E.

1925 *Spanish Exploration in the Southwest, 1542–1706.* Scribner's, New York.

1926 *Historical Memoirs of New California.* University of California Press, Berkeley.

1927 *Fray Juan Crespí, Missionary Explorer of the Pacific Coast, 1769–*

1774. University of California Press, Berkeley.

1930 *Anza's California Expeditions,* vol. IV. University of California Press, Berkele*y.*

BOOLOOTIAN, R. A.

1961 The Distribution of the California Otter. *California Fish and Game,* vol. 47, no. 3. San Francisco.

BOSCANA, GERÓNIMO

See A. Robinson (1846).

BOWERS, STEPHEN

1877 *Santa Rosa Island.* Annual Report of the Smithsonian Institution, pp. 316–320. Washington, D.C.

1883 Fish-hooks from Southern California. *Science,* o.s., vol. 1, no. 20, p. 575. Boston.

1887 Aboriginal Fish-hooks. *West American Scientist,* vol. III, no. 32, pp. 243–245. San Diego.

1897 The Santa Barbara Indians. Unpublished MS Southwest Museum, Los Angeles.

BREMMER, C. ST. J.

1932 *Geology of Santa Cruz Island, Santa Barbara County, California.* Santa Barbara Museum of Natural History, Occasional Papers, no. 1.

1933 *Geology of San Miguel Island, Santa Barbara County, California.* Santa Barbara Museum of Natural History, Occasional Papers, no. 2.

BREUIL, H.

1952 *Four Hundred Centuries of Cave Art.* Centre d'Etudes et de Documentation Prehistoriques, Montignac, Dordogne.

BRYAN, B.

1931 Excavations at Mishopsnow. *Art and Archaeology,* vol. XXXI, pp. 176–185. Baltimore and Washington.

BURKITT, M. C.

1928 *South Africa's Past in Stone and Paint.* Cambridge University Press, Cambridge, England.

CABALLERIA Y COLELL, JUAN

1892 *History of the City of Santa Barbara.*

CADZOW, D.

1934 *Petroglyphs in the Susquehanna River near Safe Harbor, Pennsylvania.* Publication of the Pennsylvania Historical Commission, vol. 3.

CAIN, H. T.

1950 *Petroglyphs of Central Washington.* University of Washington Press, Seattle.

CAUGHEY, J. W.

1933 *History of the Pacific Coast.* Lancaster Press, Los Angeles.

1952 *The Indians of Southern California in 1852.* Huntington Library, San Marino.

CESSAC, L. DE

1882*a* Rapport sur une Mission au Perou et en Californie. *Archives des Missions Scientifiques et Litteraires,* ser. 3, vol. 9, pp. 333–344. Paris.

1882*b* Observations sur des fetiches de pierre sculptes en forme de'animaux decouverts a l'île de San Nicolas (Californie). *Revue d'ethnographie,* vol. 1, pp. 30–40. Paris.

CHAPMAN, C. E.

1921 *A History of California: The Spanish Period.* The Macmillan Company, New York.

CLELAND, R. G.

1950 *This Reckless Breed of Men: The Trappers and Fur Traders of the Southwest.* Knopf, New York.

CLEMMER, J. S.

1962 *Archaeological Notes on a Chumash House Floor at Morro Bay.* Central California Archaeological Foundation, San Francisco.

COLTON, W.

1850 *Three Years in California.* Barnes, New York.

CONNER, S. W.

1962 *A Preliminary Survey of Prehistoric Picture Writing on Rock Surfaces in Central and South Central Montana.* Billings Archaeological Society, Anthropological Paper, no. 2.

COOK, S.

1940 *Population Trends Among the California Mission Indians.* University of California Press, Berkeley.

1943 *The Conflict Between the California Indians and White Civilization.* University of California Press, Berkeley.

COOKE, D. I.

1940 *Indian Trails.* Santa Barbara Museum of Natural History, Museum Talk, 15:5.

COSTANSÓ, MIGUEL

See Teggart (1911).

CRESPÍ, JUAN

See Bolton (1927).

CRESSMAN, L. S.

1937 *Petroglyphs of Oregon.* University of Oregon Publications in Anthropology, Eugene.

CUTTER, D. C.

1960 *Malaspina in California.* John Howell, San Francisco.

DAHLGREN, B., and J. ROMERO

1951 La prehistória baja california; redescubrimiento de pinturas rupestres. *Cuadernos Americanos,* 58:153–178.

DAHLGREN DE JORDAN, B.

1954 Las Pinturas Rupestres de la Baja California. *Artes de Mexico,* no. 3 (March and April).

DALTON, O. M.

1897 *Notes on the ethnographical collection from the west coast of North America (more especially in California, Hawaii and Tahiti), formed during the voyage of Captain Vancouver, 1790–1795, and now in the British Museum.* Internationale Archiv für Ethnographie, vol. 10. Leyden.

DANA, R. H.

1841 *Two Years Before the Mast,* 1941 edition. Heritage Press, New York.

DAVIDSON, D. S.

1936 *Aboriginal Australian and Tasmanian Rock Carvings and Paintings.* Memoirs of the American Philosophical Society, vol. V. Philadelphia.

DAVIS, J. T.

1961 *Trade Routes and Economic Exchange Among the Indians of California.* Reports of the California Archaeological Survey, no. 54. Berkeley.

DAVIS, W. H.

1929 *Seventy-Five Years in California.* Howell, San Francisco.

DAWSON, L., and J. DEETZ

1964 *Chumash Indian Art.* University of California at Santa Barbara.

DEETZ, J. F.

1963a *Basketry from the James-Abels Collection.* Santa Barbara Museum of Natural History, Museum Talk, vol. 38, no. 2.

1963b *Archaeological Investigations at La Purísima Mission.* University of California Archaeological Survey Annual Report, pp. 163–243. Los Angeles.

1964 A Dateable Chumash Pictograph from Santa Barbara County. *American Antiquity,* vol. 29, no. 4. University of Utah Press, Salt Lake City.

DEWDNEY, S., and KENNETH E. KIDD

1962 *Indian Rock Paintings of the Great Lakes.* University of Toronto Press.

DIESING, E. H., and F. MAGRE

1942 Petroglyphs and Pictographs in Missouri. *Missouri Archaeologist,* vol. 8, no. 1. Columbia.

DIGUET, L.

1894 Note sur la pictographie de la Basse-Californie. *Anthropologie,* 6:160–175. Paris.

1899 Rapport sur une mission scientifique dans la Basse-Californie. *Nouvelle Archives des Missions Scientifique,* no. 9, pp. 1–53. Paris.

DIXON, R. B.

1923 *The Racial History of Man.* Scribner's, New York.

DUFLOT DE MOFRAS, E.

1844 Exploration du Territoire de l'Orégon, des Californies, et de la Mer Vermeille. A. Bertrand, Paris. Reprinted in translation by Mar-

145

guerite F. Wilbur *in* Duflot de Mofras' *Travels on the Pacific Coast.* Fine Arts Press, Santa Ana, 1937.

EBERHART, H., and AGNES BABCOCK

1963 *An Archaeological Survey of Mutau Flat, Ventura County, California.* Contributions to California Archaeology, no. 5. Los Angeles.

EGENHOFF, E.

1952 Fabricas. *California Journal of Mines and Geology,* Supplement (April). San Francisco.

EISEN, GUSTAV

1904 *An Account of Indians of the Santa Barbara Islands in California.* Sitzungsberichte der königlichen Böhmischen Gesellschaft der Wissenschaften, Mathematisch-Naturwissenschaft Klasse, 1–30. Prague.

ELLISON, W. H., and FRANCIS PRICE

1953 *The Life and Adventures in California of Don Augustín Janssens.* Huntington Library, San Marino, Calif.

ELSASSER, A. B.

1955 *A Charmstone Site in Sonoma County.* Reports of the California Archaeological Survey, no. 28. Berkeley.

ELSASSER, A. B., and ROBERT HEIZER

1963 *The Archaeology of Bowers Cave, Los Angeles County.* University of California Archaeological Survey, no. 59. Berkeley.

EMMONS, G. T.

1908 Petroglyphs in Southeastern Alaska. *American Anthropologist,* 10: 221–230.

ENGERRAND, J.

1912a Nuevos Pétroglifos de la Baja California. *Boletin del Museo Nacional de Arqueologia, Historia e Etnologia,* no. 10, pp. 1–8. Mexico City.

1912b Nota Complementaria acera de los Pétroglyphos de la Baja California. *Boletin del Museo Nacional de Mexico,* no. 10. Mexico City.

ENGLEHARDT, Z.

1923 *Santa Barbara Mission.* Barry, San Francisco.

1930 *San Buenaventura.* Mission, Santa Barbara.

1932a *Mission Santa Inés.* Mission, Santa Barbara.

1932b *La Purisíma.* Mission, Santa Barbara.

1933 *San Luis Obispo.* Mission, Santa Barbara.

ERWIN, R. P.

1930 *Indian Rock Writing in Idaho.* Twelfth Annual Report, Idaho Historical Society, pp. 35–111. Boise.

FAGES, PEDRO

See Priestley (1937).

FAVOUR, A.

1936 *Old Bill Williams—Mountain Man.* University of North Carolina Press, Chapel Hill.

FENENGA, F.

1949 *Methods of recording and present status of knowledge concerning petroglyphs in California.* University of California Archaeological Survey, no. 3. Berkeley.

FERGUSSON, G. J., and W. F. LIBBY

1962 *UCLA Radiocarbon Dates II.* University of California Institute of Geophysics, Los Angeles.

1963 *UCLA Radiocarbon Dates III.* University of California Institute of Geophysics, Los Angeles.

FEWKES, J. W.

1911 *Preliminary Report on a Visit to the Navaho National Monument, Arizona.* Bureau of American Ethnology Bulletin, no. 50. Washington, D.C.

FINLEY, R. S.

1951 *Note on the Orizaba Pictograph (Olson's) Cave, Santa Cruz Island, Santa Barbara, California.* National Speleological Society, Monthly Report of the Stanford Grotto, 1:2–3. Palo Alto, Calif.

FINNERTY, P.

1964 A Burial Site in the Carrizo Plain, San Luis Obispo County, California. Unpublished MS.

FITCH, J. E.
1961 *The Pismo Clam.* Marine Resources Leaflet, no. 1. Sacramento.

FONT, PEDRO
See Bolton (1930).

FORBES, A.
1839 *A History of Upper and Lower California, North of Mexico.* Smith and Elder, London.

FORD, H. C.
1960 *Notes on Excavations Made in Indian Burial Places in Carpinteria.* Reports of the California Archaeological Survey, no. 50. Berkeley.

FREDERICK, M. C.
1901 Some Indian Paintings. *Land of Sunshine*, vol. XV, no. 4, pp. 223–227.

GARDNER, E. S.
1962a The Case of the Baja Caves. *Life*, 53:62–64.
1962b The Hidden Heart of Baja. Morrow, New York.

GATES, M. J.
1894 *Contributions to Local History. See* Latta (1949).

GATSCHET, A. S.
1879 *A Classification of Western Indian Languages.* Geographical Surveys West of the One Hundredth Meridian, vol. VII. Washington, D.C.

GAYTON, A. H.
1948 *Yokuts and Western Mono Ethnography.* University of California Anthropological Records, vol. 10. Berkeley and Los Angeles.

GEBHARD, D.
1951 Petroglyphs of Wyoming: A Preliminary Paper. *El Palacio*, vol. 58, no. 3, pp. 67–81. Santa Fe.
1954 *Petroglyphs in the Boysen Basin, Wyoming.* University of Wyoming Publication, vol. XVIII, no. 1, pp. 66–70.
1957 Pictographs in the Sierra Blanca Mountains. *El Palacio*, vol. 64, no. 3, pp. 215–222. Santa Fe.
1958a Hidden Lake Pictographs. *El Palacio*, vol. 68, no. 4, pp. 146–149. Santa Fe.
1958b Nineteen Centuries of American Abstraction. *Art News*, vol. 59, no. 10, pp. 20–23.
1960 *Prehistoric Paintings of the Diablo Region of Western Texas.* Roswell Museum Publications in Art and Science, no. 3. Roswell, N.M.
1962 Prehistoric Rock Drawings at Painted Grotto, New Mexico. *El Palacio*, vol. 69, no. 4. Santa Fe.
1963 Rock Drawings in the Western United States. *IPEK, Jahrbuch fur Prahistorische und Ethnographische Kunst*, vol. 20. Berlin.

GEBHARD, D., G. A. AGOGINO, and V. HAYNES
1964 Horned Owl Cave, Wyoming. *American Antiquity*, vol. 29, no. 3, pp. 360–368.

GEBHARD, D., and H. A. CAHN
1950 The Petroglyphs of Dinwoody, Wyoming. *American Antiquity*, vol. 15, no. 3, pp. 219–228.

GEIGER, M.
1960 *The Indians of the Santa Barbara Mission.* Mission, Santa Barbara.

GIFFORD, E. W.
1940 *California Bone Artifacts.* University of California Anthropological Records, vol. 3, pp. 153–237. Berkeley.
1947 *California Shell Artifacts.* University of California Anthropological Records, vol. 9, no. 1, pp. 1–132. Berkeley.

GJESSING, G.
1952 Petroglyphs and Pictographs in British Columbia. In *Indian Tribes of Aboriginal America.* Selected Papers of the XXIXth International Congress of Americanists, pp. 66–79.
1958 Petroglyphs and Pictographs in the Coast Salishan Area of Canada. In *Miscellanea Paul Rivet.* Publicationes del Instituto de Historia, Primera Serie, no. 50, pp. 257–275. Mexico City.

GLADWIN, H.
1947 *Men Out of Asia.* McGraw-Hill, New York.

147

1957 *A History of the Ancient Southwest.* Bond Wheelwright, Portland, Me.

GOODALL, E., C. K. COOKE, and J. D. CLARK
1959 *Prehistoric Rock Art of Central Africa.* National Publications Trust, Salisbury, Southern Rhodesia.

GRANT, C.
1960 *Prehistoric Paintings of the Santa Barbara Region.* Santa Barbara Museum of Natural History, Museum Talk, 3:29.

1961a Ancient Art in the Wilderness. *Pacific Discovery* (July–August), San Francisco.

1961b *Facsimile of Indian Pictograph in Cuyama Area.* Santa Barbara Museum of Natural History, Annual Report. Santa Barbara. P. 24.

1962a Cave Paintings of the Chumash. *Arts,* (May–June). New York.

1962b *The Carpinteria Tar Pits.* Santa Barbara Historical Society, Noticias 8:11–20. Santa Barbara.

1964a California's Painted Caves. *Desert Magazine* (May). Palm Desert, Calif.

1964b *A Collection of Chumash Artifacts from the Sierra Madre Mountains of Santa Barbara County, California.* University of California Archaeological Survey, no. 63. Berkeley.

1964c California's Legacy of Indian Rock Art. *Natural History Magazine* (June), New York.

1965 Rock Painting in California. *IPEK, Jahrbuch fur Prahistorische und Ethnographische Kunst,* vol. 21. Berlin.

GRAZIOSI, P.
1960 *Palaeolithic Art.* McGraw-Hill, New York.

GREEN, W.
1935 Cave Painting in Ventura County. Unpublished MS in author's collection.

HAMY, E. T.
1882 Rapport sur la Mission de Mm. Pinart et de Cessac dans les deux Ameriques. *Archives des Missions Scientifiques et Litteraires,* ser. 3, vol. 9, pp. 323–332. Paris.

1885 *The Fishhook Industry of the Ancient Inhabitants of the Archipelago of California. Revue d'Ethnographie,* 4:6–13. Paris.

HARRINGTON, J. P.
1928 *Exploration of the Burton Mound, Santa Barbara.* Annual Report of the Bureau of Ethnology, Washington, D.C.

1934 *A New Original Version of Boscana's Historical Account of the Indians of Southern California.* Smithsonian Institution, Miscellaneous Collections, vol. 92, no. 4.

1942 *Culture Element Distributions: XIX, Central California Coast.* University of California, Anthropological Records, 7:1–46. Berkeley.

HARRINGTON, M. R., and C. E. ROZAIRE
1958 *Arts of Southern California, IV. Prehistoric and Indigenous Indian Art.* Long Beach Museum of Art, Long Beach, Calif.

HEIZER, R. F.
1938a *The Plank Canoe of the Santa Barbara Region.* Ethnological Studies, no. 7. Gothenburg.

1938b *An Inquiry into the Status of the Santa Barbara Spear Thrower. American Antiquity,* 4:137–141.

1940a *Aboriginal Use of Bitumen by the California Indians.* California Division of Mines Bulletin, no. 118, p. 74. San Francisco.

1940b Curved Single-piece Fishhooks of Shell and Bone in California. *American Antiquity,* vol. 15, no. 2, pp. 89–97. Menasha, Wis.

1941a A California Messianic Movement of 1801 Among the Chumash. *American Anthropologist,* vol. 43, no. 1. pp. 128–129. Andover, Mass.

1941b The Direct-Historical Approach in California Archaeology. *American Antiquity,* 7:98–122. Menasha, Wis.

1945 *Honey-dew "Sugar" in Western North America. Southwest Museum Masterkey*, vol. 19, no. 5. Los Angeles.

1949 *The Archaeology of Central California, I: The Early Horizon.* University of California Anthropological Records, vol. 12, no. 1. Berkeley.

1952 *The Mission Indian Vocabularies of Alphonse Pinart.* University of California Anthropological Records, vol. 15, no. 1. Berkeley.

1953 *Sacred Rain Rocks of Northern California.* University of California Archaeological Survey, no. 20. Berkeley.

1955a *California Linguistic Records and the Mission Indian Vocabularies of H. W. Henshaw,* ed. with Ethnographic notes by R. F. Heizer. University of California Anthropological Records, vol. 15, no. 2. Berkeley.

1955b Two Chumash Legends. *Journal of American Folklore,* 68:34, 56, 72. Philadelphia.

1957 *A Steatite Whale Figurine from San Nicolás Island.* University of California Archaeological Survey, no. 38. Berkeley.

1958 *Aboriginal California and Great Basin Cartography.* University of California Archaeological Survey Report, 41:1–9. Berkeley.

1960 *Some Prehistoric Bullroarers from California Caves.* University of California Archaeological Survey Report, 50:5–9. Berkeley.

1962a *The California Indians: Archaeology, Varieties of Culture, Arts of Life. California Historical Society Quarterly,* vol. XLI, no. 1. San Francisco.

1962b *A Guide to Archaeological Field Methods,* 3rd ed. National Press, Palo Alto.

HEIZER, R. F., and M. A. BAUMHOFF
1962 *Prehistoric Rock Art of Nevada and Eastern California.* University of California Press, Berkeley.

HEIZER, R. F., and A. B. ELSASSER
1961 *Original Accounts of the Lone Woman of San Nicolás Island.* University of California Archaeological Survey, no. 55. Berkeley.

HEIZER, R. F., and H. KELLEY
1962 Burins and Bladelets in the Cessac Collection from Santa Cruz Island. *Proceedings American Philosophical Society,* vol. 106, no. 2. Philadelphia.

HEIZER, R. F., and A. E. TREGANZA
1944 Mines and Quarries of the Indians cf California. *California Journal of Mines and Geology,* Report XL, pp. 291–359. Berkeley.

HEIZER, R. F., and M. A. WHIPPLE
1951 *The California Indians.* University of California Press, Berkeley.

HENSHAW, H. W.
1885 The Aboriginal Relics Called "Sinkers" or "Plummets." *American Journal of Archaeology,* 1: 105–114. Cambridge, Mass.

See also R. F. Heizer (1955a).

HEWES, G. W.
1941 Reconnaissance of the Central San Joaquin Valley. *American Antiquity,* vol. 7, no. 2, p. 131.

HEYE, G.
1921 *Certain Artifacts from San Miguel Island.* Museum of the American Indian, Heye Foundation, Indian Notes and Monographs, 7:1–184.

1926 *Chumash Objects from a California Cave.* Museum of the American Indian, Heye Foundation, Indian Notes and Monographs, 3:193–198. New York.

HODGE, F. W.
1907 *Handbook of the American Indians North of Mexico.* Bureau of American Ethnology Bulletin, no. 30. Washington, D.C.

HOLT, W. B.
1937 *Tomolos Rode at Anchor.* Santa Barbara Museum of Natural History, Museum Talk, 12:88.

IOVIN, JUNE
1963 *A Summary of Luiseño Material*

BIBLIOGRAPHY

Culture. University of California Archaeological Survey Annual Report, 1962–1963. Los Angeles, pp. 79–134.

IRWIN, MARGARET C.
1950 *Petroglyphs Near Santa Barbara.* Santa Barbara Museum of Natural History, Museum Talk, 25: 1–5.

JACKSON, A. T.
1938 *Picture Writing of Texas Indians.* University of Texas Publication, no. 3809. Austin.

JEPSON, W. L.
1925 *Manual of the Flowering Plants of California.* Sather Gate, Berkeley.

JOHNSON, M. J., and H. J. SNOOK
1935 *Seashore Animals of the Pacific Coast.* The Macmillan Company, New York.

JOHNSTON, B. E.
1962 *California's Gabrieliño Indians.* Southwest Museum, Los Angeles.

KETTL, J. W.
1962 Project Petroglyphs. *Southwest Museum Masterkey*, vol. XXXVI (January–March). Los Angeles.

KIDDER, A. V., and S. J. GUERNSEY
1919 *Archaeological Explorations in Northwestern Arizona.* Bureau of American Ethnology Bulletin, no. 65. Washington, D.C.

KOWTA M., AND J. C. HURST
1960 *Site Ven-15: The Triunfo Rock Shelter.* University of California Archaeological Survey Annual Report, Los Angeles.

KROEBER, A. L.
1904 *The Languages of the Coast South of San Francisco.* University of California Publications in American Archaeology and Ethnology, 2:29–80.

1910 *The Chumash and Costanoan Languages.* University of California Publications in American Archaeology and Ethnology, 9: 237–271. Berkeley.

1922 *Basket Designs of the Mission Indians.* American Museum of Natural History, Anthropological Papers, 20: 149–183. New York.

1925 *Handbook of the Indians of California.* Bureau of American Ethnology Bulletin, no. 78. Washington, D.C.

1959 *Ethnographic Interpretations 7–11.* University of California Publications in American Archaeology and Ethnology, vol. 47, no. 3. Berkeley.

KROEBER, THEODORA
1961 *Ishi in Two Worlds.* University of California Press. Berkeley and Los Angeles.

LA MONK, CHARLES S.
1953 *Pictograph Cave, Burro Flats.* Archaeological Survey Association of Southern California Newsletter, vol. 1, no. 2, pp. 8–9. Los Angeles.

1954 *Painted Rock.* Archaeological Survey Association of Southern California Newsletter, vol. 2, no. 4, pp. 3–5. Los Angeles.

LATHRAP, D.
1950 *A Distinctive Pictograph from the Carrizo Plains, San Luis Obispo County.* University of California Archaeological Survey, no. 9. Berkeley.

LATTA, F. F.
1949 *Handbook of the Yokuts Indians.* Bear State Books. Oildale.

LEONARD, Z.
1839 *Narrative of the Adventures of Zenas Leonard.* Clearfield, Pa.

LHOTE, H.
1959 *The Search for the Tassili Frescoes.* Transl. by Alan H. Broderick. Dutton, New York.

LIBBY, W. F.
1955 *Radiocarbon Dating.* University of Chicago Press.

LLOYD, NANCY
1954 The Acculturation of the Chumash. Unpublished MS in the possession of Mrs. Francis V. Lloyd, Santa Barbara.

MACGOWAN, K.
1950 *Early Man in the New World.* The Macmillan Company, New York.

MALLERY, G.

1886 *Pictographs of the North American Indians.* 4th Annual Report of the Bureau of American Ethnology. Washington, D.C.

1893 *Picture Writing of the American Indians.* 10th Annual Report of the Bureau of American Ethnology. Washington, D.C.

MARTÍNEZ, JOSÉ LONGINOS

See Simpson (1961).

MCADAMS, W.

1887 *Records of Ancient Races in the Mississippi Valley.* Barns, St. Louis.

MEIGHAN, CLEMENT W.

1959 Californian Cultures and the Concept of an Archaic Stage. *American Antiquity,* 24:289–305.

MENZIES, A.

1924 Menzies' California Journal. *California Historical Society Quarterly,* 2:265–340. San Francisco.

MERRIAM, C. H.

1962 *Studies of California Indians.* University of California Press, Berkeley and Los Angeles.

MOHR, A., and L. L. SAMPLE

1955*a* Twined Water Bottles of the Cuyama Area, Southern California. *American Antiquity,* 20:345–354.

1955*b* The Religious Importance of the Swordfish in the Santa Barbara Channel Area. *Southwest Museum Masterkey,* 29:62–68. Los Angeles.

MOMYER, G.

1937 *Indian Picture Writing in Southern California.* San Bernardino.

MORRISON, A. L.

1926 The Painted Rocks of the Carisa (Carrizo Plains). *National Motorist* (January 30).

MORSS, N.

1931 *The Ancient Culture of the Fremont River in Utah.* Peabody Museum Papers, vol. XII, no. 3. Cambridge, Mass.

MOUNTFORD, C. P.

1956 Art, myth, and symbolism, in: *Records of the American-Austra-*

lian Scientific Expedition to Arnhem Land, vol. I. Melbourne.

MULLOY, W.

1958 *A Preliminary Historical Outline for the Northwest Plains.* University of Wyoming Publications, vol. 22, no. 1. Laramie.

NIDEVER, GEORGE

1937 *The Life and Adventures of a Pioneer of California Since 1834,* ed. by W. H. Ellison. University of California Press, Berkeley.

OBERMAIER, H., and P. WEINERT

1919 *Las Pinturas Rupestres del Barranco de Valltorta.* Castellon, Madrid.

OLBÉS, FATHER RAMON

See Englehardt (1930).

OLSON, R. L.

1930 *Chumash Prehistory.* University of California Publications in American Archaeology and Ethnology, vol. 28, pp. 1–21. Berkeley.

ORELLANA, R.

1953 Petroglifos y Pinturas Rupestres de Sonora. *YAN,* Organo oficial del Centro de Investigaciones antropológicas de México, vol. 1. México, D. F.

ORR, PHIL C.

1943 *Archaeology of Mescalitan Island, and Customs of the Canaliño.* Santa Barbara Museum of Natural History, Occasional Papers, no. 5.

1947 Additional Bone Artifact Types in the Santa Barbara Museum of Natural History. In Gifford (1947), 115–132.

1951 *Cave of the Killer Whales.* Santa Barbara Museum of Natural History, Museum Talk (Spring).

1952 Review of Santa Barbara Channel Archaeology. *Southwestern Journal of Anthropology,* vol. 8.

1954 *Who Painted Painted Cave?* Archaeological Survey Association of Southern California Newsletter, vol. 2, no. 2, pp. 7–8. Los Angeles.

1956*a* *Pleistocene Man in Fishbone Cave,*

BIBLIOGRAPHY

Pershing County, Nevada. Nevada State Museum Archaeological Bulletin, no. 2. Carson City.

1956b *Radiocarbon Dates from Santa Rosa Island, I.* Santa Barbara Museum of Natural History Bulletin, no. 2.

1956c *Dwarf Mammoths and Man on Santa Rosa Island.* Papers of the Third Great Basin Archaeological Conference. University of Utah Anthropology Papers, 26: 74–81. Salt Lake City.

1960 *Radiocarbon Dates from Santa Rosa Island, II.* Santa Barbara Museum of Natural History Bulletin, no. 3.

1962 *On New Radiocarbon Dates from the California Channel Islands.* Western Speleological Institute, no. 8. Carson City.

OVER, W. H.
1941 *Indian Picture Writing in South Dakota.* University of South Dakota Archaeological Circular, no. IV. Vermillion.

PAEZ, JUAN
See Bolton (1925).

PALOU, F.
See Bolton (1926).

PEITHMAN, I.
1952 Pictographs and Petroglyphs in Southern Illinois. *Journal of Illinois State Archaeological Society,* vol. 2, no. 4. Springfield.

PEPPER, CHORAL
1964 Petroglyphs, the Unsolved Mystery. *Desert Magazine* (November). Palm Desert, Calif.

PINART, A.
See Heizer (1952).

POWELL, J. W.
1891 *Indian Linguistic Families of America North of Mexico.* Seventh Annual Report, Bureau of American Ethnology, Washington, D. C.

PRENTICE, R. A.
1951 A Pictograph Story of Koñate. *El Palacio,* vol. 58 (March). Sante Fe.

PRIESTLEY, H. I., ed.
1937 *A Historical, Political, and Natural Description of California by Pedro Fages, Soldier of Spain.* University of California Press, Berkeley.

PUTNAM, F.
1879 *Reports Upon the Archaeological and Ethnological Collections from the Vicinity of Santa Barbara, California, etc.* U. S. Geographical Surveys West of the 100th Meridian, vol. VII. Washington, D.C.

REICHLEN, H., and ROBERT F. HEIZER
1963 La Mission de Léon de Cessac en Californie, 1877–79. *Objets et Mondes,* vol. III, no. 1. Paris.

REINMAN, F. M., and S. J. TOWNSEND
1960 *A Petroglyph Cave on San Nicolás Island.* University of California Archaeological Survey Annual Report. Los Angeles.

RENAUD, E. B.
1936 *Pictographs and Petroglyphs of the High Western Plains.* Archaeological Survey of the High Western Plains, 8th Report, Department of Anthropology, University of Denver.

ROBINSON, A.
1846 *Life in California Before the Conquest.* Wiley & Putnam, New York.

ROBINSON, E.
1955 *Vancouver's California Bows.* University of California Archaeological Survey, no. 28. Berkeley.

ROGERS, D. B.
1929 *Prehistoric Man of the Santa Barbara Coast.* Santa Barbara Museum of Natural History.

ROSS, E. T.
1938 A Preliminary Survey of the Petroglyphs of Southern California. Unpublished MS.

ROZAIRE, C. E.
1959 Pictographs at Burro Flats. *Ventura Historical Society Quarterly* (February).

ROZAIRE, C. E., and C. KRITZMAN
1960 A Petroglyph Cave on San Nicolás Island. *Southwest Museum*

Masterkey, vol. 34, no. 4. Los Angeles.

SAUNDERS, C. F.
1934 *Useful Wild Plants of the United States and Canada.* McBride, New York.

SCHAAFSMA, POLLY
1962 Rock Art of the Navajo Reservoir. *El Palacio*, vol. 69, no. 4. Santa Fe.

SCHUMACHER, P.
1875 The Manufacture of Shell Fishhooks by the Early Inhabitants of the Santa Barbara Channel Islands. *Archiv fur Anthropologie*, 8:223–224. Translated in University of California Archaeological Survey, 1960, no. 50, pp. 23–25.

1877 *Researches in the Kjökkenmoddings and Graves of a Former Population of the Santa Barbara Islands and the Adjacent Mainland.* Bulletin of the U. S. Geological and Geographical Survey of the Territories, 3:37–56. Washington, D.C.

1878a Ancient Olla Manufactory on Santa Catalina Island, California. *American Naturalist*, vol. XII, no. 9. Philadelphia.

1878b *The Method of Manufacture of Several Articles by the Former Indians of Southern California.* Eleventh Annual Report of the Peabody Museum of Archaeology and Ethnology. Cambridge, Mass.

SECRIST, K. G.
1960 *Pictographs in Central Montana, Part I.* Montana State University Anthropological Papers, no. 20. Missoula.

SEÑÁN, JOSÉ
See Englehardt (1930); Simpson (1962).

SIMPSON, L. B.
1961 *Journal of José Longinos Martínez: Notes and Observations of the Naturalist of the Botanical Expedition in New and Old California and the South Coast, 1791–1792.* Transl. and ed. by Lesley Byrd Simpson for the Santa Barbara Historical Society. Howell, San Francisco.

1962 *The Letters of José Señán, O.F.M.: Mission San Buenaventura, 1796–1823.* Transl. by Paul D. Nathan and ed. by Lesley Byrd Simpson for the Ventura County Historical Society. Howell, San Francisco.

SMITH, G. A., *et al.*
1961 *Indian Picture Writing of San Bernardino and Riverside Counties.* San Bernardino County Museum Association Publication, vol. 7, no. 3.

SOULÉ, F., J. H. GIHON, and J. NISBET
1854 *The Annals of San Francisco.* Appleton, New York.

STEWARD, J. H.
1929 *Petroglyphs of California and Adjoining States.* University of California Publications in American Archaeology and Ethnology, vol. 24, no. 2. Berkeley.

1933 *Ethnography of the Owens Valley Paiute.* University of California Publications in American Archaeology and Ethnology, vol. 33, no. 3, pp. 334–335. Berkeley.

1936 *Petroglyphs of the United States.* Annual Report of the Smithsonian Institution. Washington, D.C.

1941 *Archaeological Reconnaissance of Southern Utah.* Smithsonian Institution Bulletin, no. 128. Washington, D.C.

STIRLING, E. C.
1896 *Report of the Work of the Horn Scientific Expedition to Central Australia*, vol. 4. Melbourne.

STRONG, E.
1959 *Stone Age on the Columbia River.* Binfords and Mort, Portland, Ore.

STRONG, W. D.
1935 *Archaeological Exploration in the Country of the Eastern Chumash.* Exploration and Field Work of the Smithsonian Institution in

153

BIBLIOGRAPHY

1934, pp. 69–72. Washington, D.C.

STRONG, W. D., and W. E. SCHENCK
1925 Petroglyphs near the Dalles of the Columbia River. *American Anthropology*, 27:77–90.

STRONG, W. D., W. E. SCHENCK, and J. H. STEWARD
1930 *Archaeology of the Dalles-Deschutes Region*. University of California Publications in American Archaeology and Ethnology, vol. 29, no. 1. Berkeley and Los Angeles.

SUDWORTH, G. B.
1908 *Forest Trees of the Pacific Slope*. Department of Agriculture. Washington, D.C.

SWANTON, J. D.
1953 *The Indian Tribes of North America*. Bureau of American Ethnology Bulletin, no. 145. Washington, D.C.

SWIFT, R. H.
1931 *Prehistoric Paintings in Santa Barbara*. Southern California Archaeological Society Publication, no. 3, pp. 35–38.

TAPÍS, ESTÉVAN
See Englehardt (1932a).

TATUM, R. M.
1946 Distribution and Bibliography of the Petroglyphs of the United States. *American Antiquity*, vol. XII, no. 2, pp. 122–125.

TAYLOR, A. S.
1860 Indianology of California. *California Farmer and Journal of Useful Sciences*, vol. XIII–XX (Feb. 22, 1860–Sept. 11, 1863). San Francisco.

TEGGART, F. J.
1911 *The Portolá Expedition of 1769–1770: Diary of Miguel Costanso*. Publications of the Academy of Pacific Coast History, vol. II, no. 4. Berkeley.

THOMPSON, J. A.
1961 *El Gran Capitan José De la Guerra*. Franciscan Fathers of California, Los Angeles.

TREGANZA, A. E.
1942 An Archaeological Reconnaissance of Northeastern Baja California and Southeastern California. *American Antiquity*, vol. 8, no. 2, pp. 160–161.

TRUE, D. L.
1954 *Pictographs of the San Luis Rey Basin. American Antiquity*, vol. 20, no. 1, pp. 68–72.

VANCOUVER, G.
1798 *A Voyage of Discovery in the North Pacific Ocean and Round the World; In Which the Coast of North-West America Has Been Carefully Examined and Accurately Surveyed . . . Performed in the Years 1790, 1791, 1792, 1793, 1794, and 1795 in the Discovery Sloop of War and Armed Tender Chatham, Under the Command of Captain George Vancouver*. Robinson, London.

VOEGLIN, E. W.
1938 *Tubatulabal Ethnography*. University of California Anthropological Records, vol. 2, no. 1. Berkeley.

WAGNER, H. R.
1929 *Spanish Voyages to the Northwest Coast of America*. California Historical Society, San Francisco.

WALLACE, WILLIAM J.
1955 A Suggested Chronology for Southern California Coastal Archaeology. *Southwestern Journal of Anthropology*, 11:214–230. Albuquerque.

WILLOUGHBY, C. C.
1935 *Antiquities of the New England Indians*. Peabody Museum, Cambridge, Mass.

WISSLER, C.
1922 *The American Indian*. Oxford Press, New York.

WOODS, E. B.
1900 *La Piedra Pintada de la Carrisa*. Privately printed.

WOODWARD, A.
1929a Chumash Village Site Excavated. *El Palacio*, 27:224–226. Santa Fe.

154

1929*b* Shell Fishhooks of the Chumash. *Bulletin of the Southern California Academy of Sciences*, 28:41–46. Los Angeles.

1930 Shells Used by the Indians in the Village of Muwu. *Bulletin of the Southern California Academy of Sciences*, 29:105–114. Los Angeles.

1934 An Early Account of the Chumash. *Southwest Museum Masterkey*, 8:118–123. Los Angeles.

WORMINGTON, H. M.

1955 *A Reappraisal of the Fremont Culture*. Denver Museum of Natural History Proceedings, no. 1. Denver.

YANOVSKY, E.

1936 *Food Plants of the North American Indians*. Department of Agriculture, Miscellaneous Publications, no. 237. Washington, D.C.

YARROW, H. C.
See Putnam (1879).

YATES, L. G.

1889 *Charmstones or "Plummets" from California*. Annual Report of the Smithsonian Institution, pp. 296–305. Washington, D.C.

1891 *Fragments of the History of a Lost Tribe*. Reprinted 1957 from original article, University of California Archaeological Survey, no. 38. Berkeley.

1896 Indian Pictoglyphs in California. *Overland Monthly*, 2d series, 28:657–661.

Glossary

Arroba 25 pounds.

Cabalongas Seeds of the dogbane; contains strychnine and was used as a bird poison.

Calaguala acrosticum Peruvian plant of the fern family, employed as a purgative.

Canafistula The drumstick tree (*Cassia fistula*) or its pods, used as a purgative.

Comal Stone cooking slab.

Copaiba (oil) A stimulant and diuretic extracted from the *Copaifera* of South America.

Fanega 100 pounds dry measure, or about 1.6 bushels.

Gente de razón People of reason—whites.

Gentile An unconverted Indian.

Gringo A term of contempt applied to an American by California Mexicans.

Interrogatório The questionnaire sent to the various missions by the Spanish authorities in Mexico.

Mano Hand grinding stone.

Mestizo A person of mixed Spanish and Indian blood.

Neophyte A converted Indian.

Pinole Any kind of gruel or paste made of ground seeds, nuts, acorns, or the like.

Potrero An isolated grassland in the mountains.

Pueblo A town, either Indian or Spanish.

Ranchería Native village, usually of unconverted Indians.

Temescal A sweat house.

Tomol Chumash word for pine or canoe.

Tompeate A small cylindrical basket.

Vara The Spanish yard, of about 33 inches.

Index

Numbers in italics indicate pages with additional illustrations.

159

161

INDEX

The Rock Paintings of the Chumash

by CAMPBELL GRANT

Scattered through the coastal mountains of Southern California are many strangely painted caves and rocks. Reminders of the extinct Chumash Indians, the paintings until now have been little known to the general public because of their location in dense brush and mountainous terrain. During years of intensive field research, the author increased the number of known sites in the Chumash region from 19 to 80.

The paintings range in size from a few feet to more than forty feet in length, and in kind from simple line drawings in red to complex polychrome designs. Although extraordinary for their beauty alone, the pictographs were intended for more than mere decorative purposes. They probably had symbolic and religious meaning and served as shrines or as places for the performance of ritual. Dozens of reproductions of the paintings are included in the book and discussed in terms of subjects, meaning, techniques and dating.

In the field of aboriginal North American prehistoric art, the study of rock paintings has been neglected by archaeologists because of difficulties of dating the paintings or of relating them to specific cultures. In attempting to answer the questions that come to mind —Who painted them? How old are they? What do they mean?—Mr. Grant has reconstructed the way of life of their creators, whose cultural "superiority" was noted in eighteenth-century Spanish descriptions of their behavior and attitudes.

According to the distinguished American archaeologist, Robert F. Heizer, Mr. Grant's book is "the definitive work on the rock paintings of the Chumash Indians, who are the most interesting of all the California tribes, and whose cave art is the finest in North America."

Mr. Grant, an artist and the author of many articles on pictographs, is a Research Associate and Member of the Board of the Santa Barbara Museum of Natural History. A generous grant by the Museum has made possible the inclusion in the present work of the author's reproductions in color of many of the pictographs.